Seasons of the Heart

SEASONS of the HEART

INSPIRATIONAL WRITINGS OF OUR TIME

Edited by
Stephanie C. Oda

A READER'S DIGEST/C.R. GIBSON BOOK
Published by The C.R. Gibson Company, Norwalk, Connecticut 06856

CONTENTS

INTRODUCTION

Seasons of the heart come to all of us as surely as do the seasons of the year. We cannot anticipate their advent or know how long they will endure, but in the ebb and flow of every life there are seasons of love, learning, joy and hope. In living through these special times, whether they span years, days or a few fleeting hours, we are touched and inspired to grow and become the unique individuals we are.

Here is a book of seasons that we hope will inspire those who read it to reach for and savor every season of the heart. For though our seasons must pass, they stay with us always, not just as memories, but as vital parts that add up to the sum of our whole being.

SEASONS OF LOVE

FIRST LOVE

Love notes, written by Robert Frost as a boy, filled the poet with memories of a bittersweet past.

The poet Robert Frost frequently told me about his first love. She was, he said, a dark-haired, dark-eyed, mischievous tomboy. Her name was Sabra Peabody and she and Frost had been schoolmates, many years before, in Salem, N.H. As an awkward 12-year-old he wrote her ardent notes, but the young lady had many other admirers and did not encourage him. Eventually he moved away from the village and heard no more from her.

As Frost's official biographer, I mentally filed this information. But I did nothing about it until years later, when I heard that the same Sabra Peabody, now a widow, had returned to Salem to live. I wrote for an interview and received a cordial invitation from her to come to call.

I was received by a tall, lithe, vibrant woman in her 70's, white haired, and still beautiful. Her memories about the school days with Frost were much like those the elderly poet had given me. She told me how she, her brother Charles and "Rob" used to roam the woods together after school and on Saturdays. Adventurous like her brother, she used to tease Frost into keeping pace with them. She recalled that he sometimes quarreled with her over her other beaux.

I did not stay long that day, but was encouraged to return. It was during my second visit that the unexpected happened —the kind of thing biographers dream of but seldom encounter.

We had talked again, even more freely than before. Finally I stood to take my leave. Sabra remained seated. "Was there something else?" I asked. Yes, said Sabra, she had just been waiting for the right moment. She told me that this house, to which she had returned after her husband's death, had been her childhood home. Recently she had opened a dusty steamer trunk in the attic and found several family keepsakes, among them a wooden pencil box she had used in grammar-school days.

Holding it in her hand, she had suddenly remembered that in the bottom of the box there was a secret compartment which could be opened by sliding the thin wooden base outward. She tried it, the secret compartment opened, and out fell four notes, notes written by "Rob" to Sabra, perhaps in the fall of 1886. She now wanted me to see them.

As she took the notes out of a desk drawer and gave them to me, I felt great excitement in the knowledge that, almost by accident, I held the earliest known writing of a major literary figure. But as I began to read I found further rewards. "I like those leavs you gave me and put them in my speller to press," one note started out. Another pleaded: "There is no fun in getting mad every so often so lets see if we cant keep friends. . . . I like you because I cant help myself and when I get mad at you I feel mad at myself to." In such lines I could sense the rapture and the anguish of a boy in love.

The former Sabra Peabody had no idea of the importance of this find. When she offered to give me the notes, I explained that their market value was too high for me to accept them as a gift. But would she consider donating them to the collection of Robert Frost's papers at the Jones Public Library in Amherst, Mass.?

She agreed, and I delivered them a few days later to Charles R. Green, curator of the collection. Since I feared that the poet might not approve of my snooping, I asked that this gift be kept a secret. I further requested that the notes be matted, with backing, and wrapped in heavy paper; that the package be tied with string, and placed in the vault of the library with the notation "Not to be Opened During Robert Frost's Lifetime." The secret might have been preserved as planned, had not fate intervened – in the person of Robert Frost himself!

Frost had stored in that same vault a small metal strongbox containing manuscripts of some early poems. Shortly after the four notes had been turned over to the library, he appeared there unexpectedly to retrieve one of the poems. Green offered to bring the box out, but Frost said time would be saved if they both went into the vault. The poet opened his strongbox, took what he wanted, closed it – and looked around. "What's this?" he asked.

Green had inadvertently placed the secret package on a nearby shelf. Frost peered at it, then read aloud, "Not to Be Opened During Robert Frost's Lifetime." He turned accusingly to the curator. "This is your handwriting, Mr. Green."

Flustered, Green said yes, yes it was, but Larry Thompson had asked him to write it because . . .

Frost was in no mood for explanations. With clenched hands he broke the string, then tore the wrapping off the package. After reading the notes carefully, the old gentleman shoved the material back on the shelf. Then he turned and, without a word to anyone, stalked out of the library.

Green's letter of apology gave me all the details and said that the poet seemed very angry. I was worried. If Frost should not forgive me for my snooping without his permission, my work on the biography might end before it really began. What could I do to make amends? Perhaps it would be best, I decided, to let his anger cool, even to wait until *he* chose to bring up the subject. I waited.

Nothing happened until the following June when I arrived in Vermont to spend some time with the poet as he and I had planned. When I reached his farm, he was in his vegetable garden setting out a row of lettuce seedlings. His greeting was cordial and his instructions were sensible: I should take off my city jacket and prove my farming background by helping him get these plants into the ground before they began to wilt. After we finished, we went up to his cabin and sat down before the stone fireplace. Frost began to tell me how a fox had made off with one of his hens. "I didn't react fast enough," he said. "Nothing like that has happened to me since I was a boy in Salem and . . . "

Salem! Reminded of unfinished business, he stopped in the middle of the sentence. His expression changed. He leaned toward me, shook the index finger of his right hand under my nose, and said, "You! You! What *you* did to *me!*" With that he launched into his version of the visit to the Jones Library.

He said that as soon as he saw the admonition on the packet and heard Green say my name, he knew that I'd been prying. Hurt and angry that I hadn't confided in him, he had broken the string and torn open the package almost before he realized what he was doing.

The feeling of resentment had been swept away by the opening words: "Dear Sabe." No one could possibly understand, he said, how overwhelmed he was by the memories which flooded up as he read. By the time he finished the last note, he could feel the tears burning in his eyes. He couldn't bear to have Green see those tears; he couldn't talk to anyone. So he fled. When Frost paused and silence filled the room, I was the one whose eyes stung.

Then, suddenly, his manner changed and he looked me straight in the eye. "So you found her?" he asked quietly.   12

I nodded.

"Where?"

"Salem."

He continued to stare at me and I didn't dare go on. The silence became uncomfortable. Finally he spoke, almost to himself. "Sixty years!" I had to lean forward to hear him. "Sixty years . . . and I've never forgotten."

Then he leaned back. "You can start," he said quietly. "Start at the beginning and tell me all about her."

Lawrance Thompson

"ROSES ARE RED . . ."

Roses are red
Violets are blue
This is the operator
With a collect call for you.

My daughters away at college tell me almost weekly that they love me. The phone rings and I hear, "This is the operator. Will you accept a collect call?" I say yes and from the other end a voice explodes: "*Mom!* I know I shouldn't have called, but I need your help." I ask, "How much?" Sometimes they say $20, but more often, "Nothing, Mom, I just need to talk."

My youngest daughter, down through the years, has told me repeatedly she loved me . . . after laying in my arms puppies, lambs, bunnies, mice and 27 kittens, and saying, "Hold it, Ma, while I go call and say we can keep it!"

Roses are red
Violets are blue
This candy heart tells
What I think of you.

My third-grader told me he loved me today. He had a ten-cent box of candy hearts and he poured them all out on a table to read each one. He ate the "sez you," then the "love you" and the "me too," and was about to pop in the "hubba" when he paused and asked, "Mommy, what does 'hubba' mean?"

I told him it was once something you said when you thought a person was really special, very pretty and extra nice. He studied the candy heart a moment, then shoved it toward me. "Here," he said.

Roses are red
Violets are blue
If I don't say I love you
It means that I do.

After Hal and I were married, he never said he loved me anymore.

"Hal," I asked, "do you love me?" He said, "Yeah."

"How come you never tell me?" He shrugged, "I don't know."

"Hal," I persisted, "I want to tell you I love you. If you love me, I can't understand why you don't want to tell me you love me, too."

He took my hands in his hands and said, "Jo, try to understand. It's hard for me to say I love you. I don't know why. . . it's just the way I am." Then he made me a promise: "Jo, if ever I don't love you, I will tell you I don't love you. So . . . if I don't tell you I love you, you know that I do!"

JoAnn Dolan

In the all-important world of family relations,
three other words are almost as powerful
as the famous "I love you."
They are, "Maybe you're right."

Oren Arnold

AN AFFAIR BY PHONE

It was a most unusual way to fall in love. But the language of words is more powerful than that of the eyes.

In September 1941, after having been wounded in a bombing raid on London, I was discharged from the hospital. My military career had been inglorious. I was disappointed with myself, and deeply depressed by the turn the war had taken. Fortunately, at this time I was sustained by the most intimate and delicious friendship of my life.

Late one night in London, I was trying to telephone a friend. Instead of getting through to him my line was crossed with that of a woman, also wanting to telephone. "My number is Grosvenor 8829," I heard her tell the operator, "and I want a Hampstead number. Instead, you have hitched me up to Flaxman something in Chelsea. This poor man doesn't want to talk to me at all."

"Oh, yes, I do, " I joined in, for I liked her voice immensely. It was harmonious and clever. Instead of being cross, this woman was very good-humored about the muddle. After mutual apologies we both hung up. A minute or two later I dialed again, and again got on to her, although there was no resemblance between her number and the one I was trying to get.

Since it seemed that our lines were destined to link up, we talked for 20 minutes. "Why were you wanting to speak to a friend after midnight, anyway?" she asked. I told her the reason, which I have now forgotten. "And why were you?" I asked her. She explained that her old mother slept badly, and she often talked to her late at night. Then we discussed the books we were reading, and of course the war. Finally I said, "I don't remember enjoying a talk so much for years."

"It was fun, wasn't it? Well, I suppose we ought to stop now," she said. "Good-night. Pleasant dreams."

All next day I thought of our conversation, of her intelligence, her spontaneity, her enthusiasm, her sense of fun. I thought too of her distinctive accent, which was soft and seductive, without being the least insinuating. Its musical modulation haunted me.

That evening in bed I paid little attention to what I was reading. By midnight, Grosvenor 8829 was recurring so often in my head that I could bear it no longer. I got up, and with trepidation dialed the number. I heard the swift, disengaged purr of the bell at the other end. The receiver there was picked up instantly. "Hello!"

"It's me," I said. "Sorry to be a bore, but may we continue our conversation where we left off last night?" Without saying no or yes, she launched upon a funny and original dissertation on Balzac's *La Cousine Bette*. Within minutes we were joking and laughing as though we had known each other for years.

This time we talked for three-quarters of an hour. She was enchanting. The late hour and our anonymity broke down all those absurdly conventional reserves which usually hedge two people during preliminary meetings after an introduction. But when I suggested that we ought to introduce ourselves, she would not have it. It might spoil everything, she said. Her only concession was to make a note of my telephone number.

I did extract a promise from her that we would reveal our identities when the war ended. I learned that she had been married at 17 to a disagreeable man from whom she was separated. She was 36. Her only child had recently been killed flying at the age of 18. Since she once described him as being beautiful as the dawn, and another time as resembling her in every feature, I had a picture of her which never changed. When I told her how beautiful she was to contemplate, she merely laughed and asked, "How do you know I am?"

We grew to depend upon each other. There were no subjects we did not discuss. Our views on most were identical, including those on the war. She gave me counsel and strength. Never a night passed when we were both in London that we did not telephone, no matter how late. I would look forward to our next talk the whole preceding day. If I went away for the weekend and was unable to telephone she complained that she could hardly get to sleep for loneliness.

At times I found it unbearable not to see her. I would threaten to jump into a taxi and drive to her at once, but she would not give in — she said that if we met and found we did not love, as then we did, it would kill her. Whenever there was a bad raid at night I would ring up, after it was over, to find out how she was. This always amused her. But I noticed that whenever she imagined there was one over Chelsea she did the same.

For 12 months I lived in an extraordinary state of inner content — extraordinary because the times through which we were living were grim, and our love was in a sense unfulfilled. But it had compensations; our passage was entirely free from the usual shoals and reefs that beset the turbulence of passion, and there seemed no reason why it should not flow on this even course forever. After all, the language of words is more powerful and more lasting than that of the eyes, or the hands.

But fate struck swiftly. One night I got back to London late from the country. I picked up the receiver and dialed her number. Instead of the clear, healthy ringing tone or the high-pitched engaged signal, there was a prolonged, piercing scream. I can never listen to that signal now without feeling faint. It means the line is out of order or no longer exists.

Next day the same scream was repeated. And the next. In distress I asked Information to find out what had happened.

At first Information would say nothing. They thought it odd that I could not even tell them the subscriber's name. Finally an obliging operator agreed for once to disregard 18 regulations. "Why not?" she said. "We may all be blown sky high any moment. And you seem worried. The fact is that the house to which this number belonged received a direct hit three days ago. There can be no harm now in giving you the subscriber's name."

"Thank you for your help," I said. "I would much rather you didn't. Please, please don't." And I rang off.

James Lees-Milne

*We love because
it's the only true adventure.*

Nikki Giovanni

A GIFT FOR MOTHER'S DAY

The family had just moved to Rhode Island, and the young woman was feeling a little melancholy on that Sunday in May. After all, it was Mother's Day — and 800 miles separated her from her parents in Ohio.

She had called her mother that morning to wish her a happy Mother's Day, and her mother had mentioned how colorful the yard was now that spring had arrived. As they talked, the younger woman could almost smell the tantalizing aroma of purple lilacs hanging on the big bush outside her parents' back door.

Later, when she mentioned to her husband how she missed those lilacs, he popped up from his chair. "I know where we can find all you want," he said. "Get the kids and c'mon."

So off they went, driving the country roads of northern Rhode Island on the kind of day only mid-May can produce: sparkling sunshine, unclouded azure skies and vibrant newness of the green and growing all around. They went past small villages and burgeoning housing developments, past abandoned apple orchards, back to where trees and brush have devoured old homesteads.

Where they stopped, dense thickets of cedars and junipers and scrub birch crowded the roadway on both sides. There wasn't a lilac bush in sight.

"Come with me," the man said. "Over that hill is an old cellar hole, from somebody's farm of years ago, and there are lilacs all around it. The man who owns this land said I could poke around here anytime. I'm sure he won't mind if we pick a few lilacs."

Before they got halfway up the hill, the fragrance of the lilacs drifted down to them, and the kids started running. Soon, the mother began running, too, until she reached the top.

There, far from view of passing motorists and hidden from

encroaching civilization, were the towering lilac bushes, so laden with the huge, cone-shaped flower clusters that they almost bent double. With a smile, the young woman rushed up to the nearest bush and buried her face in the flowers, drinking in the fragrance and the memories it recalled.

Carefully, she chose a sprig here, another one there, and clipped them with her husband's pocket knife. She was in no hurry, relishing each blossom as a rare and delicate treasure.

Finally, though, they returned to their car for the trip home. While the kids chattered and the man drove, the woman sat smiling, surrounded by her flowers, a faraway look in her eyes.

When they were within three miles of home, she suddenly shouted to her husband, "Stop the car. Stop right here!"

The man slammed on the brakes. Before he could ask her why she wanted to stop, the woman was out of the car and hurrying up a nearby grassy slope with the lilacs still in her arms.

At the top of the hill was a nursing home and, because it was such a beautiful spring day, the patients were outdoors strolling with relatives or sitting on the porch.

The young woman went to the end of the porch, where an elderly patient was sitting in her wheelchair, alone, head bowed, her back to most of the others. Across the porch railing went the flowers, into the lap of the old woman. She lifted her head and smiled.

For a few moments, the two women chatted, both aglow with happiness, and then the young woman turned and ran back to her family.

As the car pulled away, the woman in the wheelchair waved, and clutched the lilacs.

"Mom," the kids asked, "who was that? Why did you give her our flowers? Is she somebody's mother?"

The mother said she didn't know the old woman. But it was Mother's Day, and she seemed so alone, and who wouldn't be cheered by flowers? "Besides," she added, "I have all of you, and I still have my mother, even if she is far away. That woman needed those flowers more than I did."

This satisfied the kids, but not the husband. The next day he purchased half a dozen young lilac bushes and planted them around their yard, and several times since then he has added more.

I know. I was that man. The young mother was, and is, my wife.

Now, every May, our own yard is redolent with lilacs. Every Mother's Day our kids gather purple bouquets. And every year I remember that smile on a lonely old woman's face, and the kindness that put the smile there.

Ken Weber

Some people strengthen the society
just by being the kind of people they are.

John W. Gardner

A BRIGHT AND BEAUTIFUL
CHRISTMAS

A visit to a goat helps James Herriot rediscover the Christmas spirit . . .

Christmas Eve that year was a culmination of all the ideas I had ever held about Christmas—a flowering of emotions I had never experienced. It had been growing in me since the afternoon, when I went on call to a tiny village where the snow lay deep on the single street. When I returned to my home village of Darrowby, it was dark, and around the marketplace the little shops were bright with decorations and the light from their windows fell in a soft yellow wash over the trodden snow of the cobbles. People, anonymously muffled, were hurrying about; doing last-minute shopping.

As I walked, the snow crunching under my feet, the church bells clanging, the sharp air tingling in my nostrils, the wonder and mystery of Christmas enveloped me in a great wave. Peace on Earth, Goodwill Toward Men—the words became meaningful as never before and I saw myself suddenly as a tiny particle in the scheme of things; Darrowby, the farmers, the animals and I seemed for the first time like a warm, comfortable entity.

There wouldn't be much work tomorrow; we'd have a long lie—maybe till nine—and then a lazy day, a glorious hiatus in our busy life.

But at 6 a.m., the phone rang. I lifted the receiver.

"Is that the vet?"

"Yes, Herriot speaking," I mumbled.

"This is Brown, Willet Hill. I've got a cow down with milk fever. I want you here quick." Then a click at the far end.

No "Sorry to get you out of bed" or anything else, never mind "Merry Christmas." It was a bit hard.

Mr. Brown was waiting for me in the darkness of the farmyard. He didn't say good morning, but nodded briefly, then jerked his head in the direction of the barn. "She's in there."

He watched in silence as I gave the injection, and it wasn't until I was putting the bottles away that he spoke.

"I'll give you another ring if she's not up by dinner-time. And there's one other thing—that was a heck of a bill I had from you fellers last month, so tell your boss not to be so savage with 'is pen." Then he turned and walked quickly toward the house.

Well, that was nice, I thought as I drove away. A sudden wave of anger surged in me. Mr. Brown had doused my festive feeling as effectively as if he had thrown a bucket of water over me.

As I mounted the steps to my home, the morning darkness had paled to a shivery gray. Helen met me in the passage.

"I'm sorry, Jim," she said. "There's another urgent job. It's old Mr. Kirby. He's worried about his nanny goat."

Mr. Kirby was a retired farmer who had kept enough stock to occupy his time. His cottage was in a village high up the dale. He met me at the gate.

"Ee, lad," he said. "I'm right sorry to be bothering you this early in the morning and Christmas an' all, but Dorothy's real bad."

He led the way to a pen where a large white goat peered out at us anxiously. As I watched her, she gulped, gave a series of retching coughs, then stood trembling, saliva drooling from her mouth.

We went into the pen, and as the old man held the goat against the wall I tried to open her mouth. She didn't like it very much and, as I pried her jaws apart, she startled me with a loud, long-drawn, human-sounding cry. I poked a finger deep in the pharynx.

After a few minutes I turned to the farmer. "You know, this is a bit baffling. I can feel something in the back of her throat, but it's soft—like cloth. I'd been expecting to find a bit of twig, or something sharp. But if it's cloth, what the heck is holding 24 it there? Why hasn't she swallowed it?"

As I spoke, Dorothy began a paroxysm of coughs that seem-ed almost to tear her apart.

I once more pulled the goat's mouth open and again heard the curious childlike wailing. It was when the animal was in full cry that I noticed something under the tongue—a thin, dark band.

"I can see what's holding the thing now," I cried. "It's hooked round the tongue with a string or something." Carefully I pushed my forefinger under the band and began to pull.

It wasn't string. It began to stretch as I pulled carefully at it—like elastic. Then it stopped stretching, and I felt a real resistance; whatever was in the throat was beginning to move. Very slowly the mysterious obstruction came sliding up. When it came within reach, I let go of the elastic, grabbed the sodden mass and hauled it forth. It seemed as if there were no end to it—a snake of dripping material nearly two feet long—but at last I had it out onto the straw of the pen.

Mr. Kirby seized it and held it up. As he unraveled the mass wonderingly, he gave a sudden cry. "God 'elp us, it's me sum-mer drawers!"

"Your what?"

"Me summer drawers. Missus was havin' a clear-out afore the end of t' year and she didn't know whether to wash 'em or mek them into dusters. She washed them, and Dorothy must have got 'em off the line."

He held up the tattered drawers and regarded them rueful-ly. Then his body began to shake silently, a few low giggles escaped from him and finally he gave a great shout of laughter. It was an infectious laugh and I joined in. He went on for quite a long time and when he had finished he was leaning weakly against the wire netting.

"Me poor awd drawers," he gasped, then leaned over and patted the goat's head. Then, seizing my arm, he invited me into his cottage for a bit of Christmas cake.

Inside the tiny living room, I was ushered to the best chair by the fireplace where two rough logs blazed and crackled. "Bring cake out for Mr. Herriot, Mother," the farmer cried as he rummaged in the pantry. His wife bustled in carrying a cake thickly laid with icing and ornamented with colored spangles, toboggans, reindeer.

"You know, Mother," Mr. Kirby said, "we're lucky to have such men as this to come out on a Christmas mornin' to help us."

"Aye, we are that." The old lady cut a thick slice of the cake and placed it on a plate.

Cake on knee, I looked across at the farmer and his wife who were sitting in upright kitchen chairs watching me with quiet benevolence. The two faces had something in common—a kind of beauty. You would find faces like that only in the country; deeply wrinkled and weathered, clear-eyed, alight with a cheerful serenity.

"A happy Christmas to you both," I said.

The old couple nodded and replied smilingly, "And the same to you, Mr. Herriot."

"Aye, and thanks again, lad," said Mr. Kirby. "We're right grateful to you for runnin' out here to save awd Dorothy."

As I looked around the little room with the decorations hanging from the low-beamed ceiling, I could feel the emotions of last night surging slowly back. At last, I had found Christmas and peace and goodwill.

James Herriot

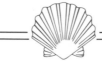

SEASONS OF LEARNING

THE SUMMMER I LEARNED TO SEE

A wise grandmother opens a small girl's eyes to the treasures around them.

It was a sticky end-of-summer dog day in Missouri. Bottom land was crazy-cracked. Heat came down like a hot skullcap, and the only sound under the brassy sky was the lonesome locust hum. I was preparing to go after the mail about a mile's distance, through fields and thickets, across creeks and a river, from our farmhouse, in which three generations of my family lived.

"Take the bucket with you," my grandmother said, handing me the very familiar half-gallon syrup bucket.

"What for?" I asked, petulantly. The berries had been picked, and it was too early for wild grapes, too late for roasting ears.

"You'll find something to fill it with," she said, her blue eyes sparkling with anticipation.

I didn't want to take the bucket. It would be a hindrance to me. I might want to skip rocks on the river, or wade in the spring branch. I was nine years old, and I'd had to carry a bucket a good portion of my life. Twice a day I'd lugged a pail for milking. With it I'd carried feed to the chickens, salt to the cows, molasses to the neighbors. Some days it seemed as if a bucket were an appendage growing out of my aching palm.

Nevertheless, I took the bucket. Halfway to the mail-box, I set it down beneath a pokeberry bush. I needn't carry it the whole way, I reasoned.

There was no mail, and nobody at the cluster of mail-boxes to talk to. A dust devil moved across a distant field, and I wished I were in the middle of it — to have my shirt puffed up and my hair blown about.

When I got back to the bucket, I saw that a few ripe poke-berries had fallen into it. With childish ill humor, I picked off enough clusters to fill the pail, even though I thought they were good for nothing.

"Aren't they just lovely!" Grandma exclaimed admiringly when I set them on the kitchen table. "We'll make some pokeberry ink." She brought a container, filled one of Grandpa's little tobacco sacks with berries and squeezed out the juice. We used the lovely magenta ink to paint intricate rings on our fingers and pen letters to distant cousins.

When I went to mail the letters the next day, Grandma again told me to take the bucket along. The sultry heat hadn't changed. Its haze simmered up ahead of me around the limp ragweed and drying foxtail. Hot dust squirted up between my bare toes. I carried the bucket a little farther than the previous day before setting it down.

There was only a sale catalogue in the mail. When I got back to the bucket, I dropped it in. But I felt vaguely uncomfortable, remembering the pokeberries. I caught sight of a clump of peppermint growing close to the path. Funny, I had passed it every day and never noticed it before. Peppermint just doesn't spring up overnight. I picked a bucketful, its pungent aroma seeming to cool the day.

Grandma was pleased with the peppermint. She liked to chew it, make tea with it, crush it in her hands. 28

The daily admonition to take the bucket along was repeated for several weeks, and I began to see other things. How long had that jewelweed been in bloom along the riverbank? How long had the abandoned oriole's nest dangled from the high elm limb?

One day, through the blue mist that gathered on our hillsides in late summer, I saw something brilliantly red. I found it to be a clump of sumac, shaped like a big, open umbrella waiting for autumn rain. When I described it to Grandma, she looked at me a long time and chuckled. "A red umbrella, eh?" Somehow I knew I'd pleased her more about the sumac than with the bucket of pennyroyal I'd brought home for the dog pens.

Then, for the first time, I noticed the monarch-butterfly migration. Dozens and dozens of monarchs drifted over, bright orange and black will-o'-the-wisps, with all the time in the world to get where they wanted to go. As I watched, it seemed that I myself had emerged from some cramped chrysalis to free and airy flight. When I finally went home, I didn't have anything in the bucket. "I forgot about it when I saw the butterflies," I told Grandma.

The next day, when I picked up the bucket before leaving for the mailbox, Grandma's hand closed over mine and gently loosened my hold. "Honey," she said, "you don't need the bucket anymore."

Jean Bell Mosley

Maturity begins to grow
when you can sense your concern for others
outweighing your concern for yourself.

John MacNaughton

A FOOTBALL FOR GRANDMA

An unusual gift becomes a grandmother's treasure and a father's inspiration.

"DaddydaddydaddyDADDY!"

That's how it came out—one long, excited word. He started yelling it at the top of the stairs, and by the time he bounded into the living room he really had it going good. I'd been talking to his mother about a money problem, and it stopped me mid-sentence.

"Robbie, *please!*" I said. Then I appealed to my wife. "Can't we have just five minutes around here without kids screaming?"

Robbie had been holding something behind his back. Now he swung it around for me to see, "Daddy, *look!*"

It was a picture, drawn in the messy crayon of a seven-year-old. It showed a weird-looking creature with one ear three times as big as the other, one green eye and one red; the head was pear-shaped, and the face needed a shave.

I turned on my son. "Is *that* what you interrupted me for? Couldn't you wait? I'm talking to your mother about something *important!*"

His face clouded up. His eyes filled with bewilderment, rage, then tears. "Awright!" he screamed, and threw the picture to the floor. "But it's *your* birthday Saturday!" Then he ran upstairs.

I looked at the picture on the floor. At the bottom, in Robbie's careful printing, were some words I hadn't noticed: MY DAD by Robert Sherman.

Just then Robbie slammed the door of his room. But I heard a different door, a door I once slammed—25 years ago—in my grandmother's house in Chicago.

It was the day I heard my grandmother say she needed   30

a *football*. I heard her tell my mother there was going to be a party tonight for the whole family, and she had to have a football, for after supper.

I couldn't imagine *why* Grandmother needed a football. I was sure she wasn't going to play the game with my aunts and uncles. She had been in America only a few years, and still spoke with a deep Yiddish accent. But Grandma wanted a football, and a football was something in *my* department. If I could get one, I'd be important, a contributor to the party. I slipped out the door.

There were only three footballs in the neighborhood, and they belonged to older kids. Homer Spicer wasn't home. Eddie Polonsky wouldn't sell or rent, at any price. The last possibility was a tough kid we called Gudgie. It was just as I'd feared. Gudgie punched me in the nose. Then he said he would trade me his old football for my new sled, plus all the marbles I owned.

I filled Gudgie's football with air at the gas station. Then I sneaked it into the house and shined it with shoe polish. When I finished, it was a football worthy of Grandmother's party. All the aunts and uncles would be proud. When nobody was looking I put it on the dining-room table. Then I waited in my room for Grandma to notice it.

But it was Mother who noticed it. "Allan!" she shouted.

I ran to the dining room.

"You know your grandmother's giving a party tonight. Why can't you put your things where they belong?"

"It's not mine," I protested.

"Then give it back to whoever it belongs to. Get it out of here!"

"But it's for Grandma! She said she needed a football for the party." I was holding back the tears.

Mother burst into laughter. "A *football* for the party! Don't you understand your own grandma?" Then, between peals of laughter, Mother explained: "Not football. FRUIT BOWL! Grandma needs a FRUIT BOWL for the party."

THE GRASS CATCHER

A father and son rediscover each other as the old man shares his secret—how to turn a humdrum task into high adventure.

I remember the day I hit upon the idea. I was driving toward my parents' house, puzzling over what I could get my father for his birthday. The pruning pole had been my outstanding choice to date. Sweaters stayed folded in drawers, books unread on the shelves, a painting kit untried in the garage, but the pruning pole showed the scars of much use and my father seemed ever grateful for it. I had even contemplated getting him a new one, but knew he would never touch it until the old one had completely disintegrated. At 75, he rebelled against discarding anything simply because it was old.

In the middle of my gift contemplations, I noticed a boy mowing his lawn. Like nine out of ten hand mowers, his had a grass catcher. I suddenly realized who owned the tenth lawn mower—my father.

Every other Saturday morning, he would mow his large front lawn. If I came by at about 10:30, as I often did, he'd be just to the pine tree, and would have from there to the hedge left to do. I'd have coffee and chat with my mother while he finished mowing and raking up the grass.

Now he would no longer have to push those long lines of grass about. I would buy a grass catcher. I knew better than to think he'd go for a noisy gasoline-powered mower, but this was different—something he could really use. I liked that. I had taken after my mother in that regard, we liked efficiency, order and practicality.

My father was another sort altogether. Driving to our vacation home, he took scenic back roads that lengthened the trip by half an hour. When we were children, he told us that there were trolls under all bridges, dwarfs in the light signals, and angels' tears in rain. When we went on walks, and we often did, we were not people walking but a band of Vikings, or Kit Carson and his explorers, or big-game hunters.

While his gift of pretending provided us with endless joy as kids, it seemed less appropriate as we grew into maturity. He became more subdued. Yet the magic between him and children remained. When I arrived for his birthday, my sister's little boys were visiting, and I saw the wild imagination surface. After he had unwrapped the grass catcher, he unhesitatingly placed the bright canvas bag on his head and became a sheik . . . a covered wagon . . . then, lowering it under his chin, a pelican. The children squealed with delight.

I watched his eyes to see if I had repeated my pruning-pole success. I hadn't. Oh, there were thanks, and questions about installation, and a certain degree of feigned enthusiasm, but I had somehow, inexplicably, missed the mark.

The next Saturday morning I found my father humming happily, pushing his old hand mower along, grass-catcherless, as though I had given him a sweater for his birthday. He had difficulty attaching the gadget, he said when I asked. So while he watched and told me tales of early San Francisco, I bolted the grass catcher to the mower and tried it out. It worked perfectly. I beamed at him, and he smiled back at me and said he was anxious to try it out. I was not convinced.

By chance, I had to drive past my parents' house on a Friday evening two weeks later. As I did, I noticed something odd. My father was mowing the lawn. On a Friday night. At six o'clock. *Without* the grass catcher.

My curiosity was intensified when, the next morning, I arrived on schedule at my parents' house and from behind the hedge my father appeared, pushing along the mower—with grass catcher attached! Only a three-foot-square patch of grass remained uncut and he matter-of-factly cut through it. The grass catcher had been so efficient, my father explained, that he had finished 15 minutes earlier than usual. He opened up the grass catcher to reveal a dense pile of grass cuttings, and smiled proudly at me.

I resolved to drop by soon and "accidentally" find my father mowing, to put an end to his need for this Saturday-morning charade. So, on Friday evening, two weeks later, I drove over.

As I pulled up to the curb, my father was pushing the mower in the far corner of the yard, his back turned to me. As I came close to the hedge, I noticed the three-foot-square patch of grass left uncut. When he saw me he stopped short, and his face reddened. He began some halfhearted explanation. Then I laughed and so did he. He beckoned me across the lawn to show me something.

A long line of grass cuttings stretched nearly across the width of the yard. Opposite it in the center of the lawn was a small pile of grass, flanked by four smaller piles. My father asked me what I saw. Piles of grass, I said. And what did they remind me of? I drew a blank. He hesitated a moment, then scrutinized me thoroughly: I felt like a piece of pyrite being appraised by a goldsmith. Then he pointed. "That pile over on the right," he said, "is Blücher. The left side is Wellington. Close in there . . ."

"The acacia droppings?"

"Yes, that's Uxbridge's cavalry. Right in front of us is Marshal Ney. The Corporal's at our rear."

"Napoleon?"

"Right," responded my father, keeping his eyes closely on the battlefield as any general would.

In the next few moments, I saw the Battle of Waterloo miraculously unfold before me. With a sweep of his rake my father would flank with the Scottish dragoons, or charge Erlon's troops into the opposition. I had read about warfare, and as an ROTC cadet had participated in mock martial exercises, but there on my father's front lawn for the first time I felt the thrill of battle. My heart sank when Ney called for

36

reinforcements and Napoleon refused. "He's finished," I said aloud.

"In history, yes," said my father, "but this is *my* battlefield." And suddenly Napoleon threw the entire Imperial Guard into the fray, and Ney broke through Wellington's center, blasting the allied armies into fragments. The French held the field, resplendent in their green uniforms.

Then, as quickly as it had begun, the vision dissolved and my father, perhaps a bit embarrassed by his own enthusiasm, began raking the grass into a large pile. I recalled the many times I had watched him fiddle with long lines of grass, making illogical piles here and there, always raking toward the center—the humdrum task turned into an adventure. I was sad that I had never known, and disappointed that I had so long ago lost my own capacity to suspend reality.

I looked over at my father. He was about to pour an armful of grass into the garbage can when I blurted out, "Let's do Custer's Last Stand!"

For a long moment my father looked into my eyes—looking for a little boy he had lost long ago. Then he pointed toward the pine tree and said, "Little Bighorn," to the apple tree, "Crow village," to the hedge . . . but before he could finish, I interrupted, "Major Reno." And my mother shook her head in perplexity as she gazed out the window and watched a father and son begin all over again.

Thomas Fitzpatrick III

GIFT FROM THE ATTIC

A journey through old memories ends in a new and startling discovery.

It happened years ago, when I was in an early stage of grandmotherhood. Yet I remember everything about that long, overly sentimental afternoon.

I sat on a rolled-up rug in the attic with my back against the chimney and contemplated the hugeness of the task I'd set for myself. The moving men were nearly through, and the rest of our sprawling two-story Alabama house was empty of furniture—indeed, empty of all else except echoes.

Only in the attic were there still things, stacks and piles of them. For more than 30 years—the 21 years of my marriage and the decade the children and I had stayed on in the house after Norman died—those things had been coming up the stairs.

Now that the children were on their own, the old place had grown too big for just me, and we were selling it. All the accumulation had to be gone through before the movers came for their final haul the next day.

I was alone under the eaves. Already I had to admit to myself that the excuse I'd given for revisiting the attic was a sham. My real reason, I knew only too well, was to bid a private and painful good-by to some things that reminded me of times when I, like they, had been a lot more in demand. Still, I really expected to find at least one or two items worth keeping or passing on to the children or grandchildren.

As a starter, I unrolled the rug I'd been sitting on. A lump rose in my throat. The first rug Norman and I had bought, it was a reminder of the lean, hectic early years of marriage we had loved, and somehow survived, together. But for all my efforts to keep the old imitation Persian as decent as possible until we could get a better one, it now held, only too plainly, a record of unhousebroken puppies, of babies whose rubber pants had not always been adequate, and of the shoe polish (spilled when I hurled it in a fit of temper) that had defied all cleaning fluids. Who would want it now?

The antlered deer's head leering from a corner had arrived in the same era—the trophy of a hunter husband who assumed I'd be as delighted as he to hang it over the living-room mantel. I'd hated it there, but (I recalled with a warm surge of self-congratulation) I'd never told him so. And, in fact (as part of growing up as a wife), I had rather cheerfully endured the atrocity for five years. Then we hung it in Little Norman's room where his friends so admired it that I'd actually come to enjoy its glassy-eyed stare for another ten years.

Rewarding memories. But, long ago, the old stag's head had become so shriveled and shabby that even Little Norman had tucked it out of sight. So, certainly, it was worthless to anyone.

My eye fell on the big, homemade doll house. For a moment it seemed a real possibility as a gift for one of my granddaughters, but I quickly dismissed the thought. It was far too plain and clumsily constructed to be a proper home for the plastic glamour of today's dolls. The toy house touched me only because it had been the last Santa Claus item Norman and I had made with our own hands and put under the tree together. It was of value only to me, and I had no room for it in the small apartment where I'd soon be living alone.

Useless, too, except for wringing my heart a bit, was the absurdly small Indian costume I pulled from the humpbacked trunk. I'd made it for Merrily's first-grade play. Had it been worth all that work to dress up one tiny girl to say just two words, "Welcome, Tecumseh"? Yes, I decided, recalling Merrily's inordinate pride in her "role." For that I would have done twice the work.

Norman and I had been so needed then, so indispensable, and so many things in the attic were testaments to that fact. How could I throw them all away?

Two hours passed, then three, and still I failed to find anything I could sensibly justify holding on to. Who needed the small rusty bicycle with bent handlebars and flat tires? Or the hobbyhorse that had lost its mane and tail? Or the trunkful of scarred and broken dolls?

And—here it came, the self-pity I had been working up to all afternoon—who really needed *me* anymore? The tears, dammed up for hours, burst in a flood. Like everything else in the attic, I, too, was pretty well used-up and worn-out. The best part of my life was finished! I sobbed with soul-racking abandon.

Finally, to try to get hold of myself, I went to the window and gulped in the cool, bracing air. I don't know how long I stood there feeling the absolute quiet of the empty house, and thinking how strange and sad it was that the sounds of children playing wafted up not from our lawn but from other lawns down the block. Outside, the twilight deepened in the oaks. It would soon be dark.

Then happened the brief, quick series of events that changed my thinking. A car pulled up in front of the house, and a young man and woman and four children piled out. So absorbed was I in my thoughts that it was a moment or two before I recognized them as my son, Norman, Jr., with his two children, and my older daughter, Merrily, with her two.

At the same instant, a second car, coming too fast, bore down on them. Out of long habit, I was about to yell, "Watch out for the little ones!" But I quelled the impulse, realizing there was no need for me to shout orders. Norm scooped up one child with a practiced hand while deftly herding another child safely to the curb, and Merrily handled her two children with the same efficiency.

But there was a stranger reason why I didn't shout a warning. Up there in the darkening attic I felt in that moment almost as detached from the scene below as if I had been looking down from another planet. It was this odd sense of detachment, I'm sure, that let me see things in a new and clear light. My son wasn't "Little" Norman anymore. Tall and broad of shoulder, he was the picture of strength and confidence. It was startling to see how knowing he had grown in 28 years, and to realize what a competent mother Merrily had become. My younger daughter, Gerry, just married, was quite capable of running her own life, too, without promptings from me.

The truth dawned: if I never rejoined the familiar scene below, my children and grandchildren were now quite all right without me.

Suddenly, the tears came rushing again, but for a different reason. Now I was crying for joy. I had made the great and comforting discovery that, while being indispensable is a wonderful thing at the proper time, being no longer indispensable—because one has handled the irrevocable past well or luckily enough—can bring a far greater sense of satisfaction and triumph. And then and there I knew it was time for me to step from center-stage. I had earned the privilege of relinquishing the starring role.

Norm's familiar whistle-call came from downstairs. I managed to compose myself before his head emerged through the trapdoor.

"Well, Mother, have you finished?" He switched on the light, and I saw the astonishment on his face. "What's wrong, you haven't put anything aside?" he asked. "Did you decide to throw it all out?"

"I think that should be your decision," I heard myself saying—"yours and Merrily's and Gerry's." For the first time I felt the elation of one who has truly and happily retired.

Norm said, "But didn't you find *anything* worth keeping?"

"Oh, yes," I answered. And to this day we've kept it—our priceless gift from the attic—and I don't know of any better present my family and I could have. For, since that afternoon, I've allowed them, and they've allowed me, plenty of room for independence and privacy, the kind of freedom in which respect and love can breathe and last and grow.

Ethel Salter Gayle

When I am going out for an evening I arrange the fire in my stove so that I do not fail to find a good one when I return, though it would have engaged my frequent attention had I been present. Sometimes, when I know I am to be home, I make believe I may go out and I build my best fire. And this is the art of living, too—to leave our life in a condition to go alone, and not to require a constant supervision. We will then sit down serenely to live, as by the side of a stove.

Henry David Thoreau

MORE PRECIOUS THAN PEARLS

A boy loses his most treasured possession and learns a valuable lesson in life.

I am always going back to see if the big, black clams still cluster along the clay bottoms of the winding Rock River, in southern Wisconsin, hoping to find one with a pearl luminous as the moon. It is an unfinished piece of business which has been smoldering like gold fever since the day when I, a ten-year-old, sun-dried crisp of a boy, felt with my questing thumb through a mess of clam meat and juice, touched the first hard nubbin of pearl, and turned it to the light where it flashed pale pink and white and light blue in the blazing sun.

In that instant I was caught up and consumed by the promise of such riches as all prospectors must dream about. I became feverish with anticipation, and I could understand the visions that compelled prospectors to die crossing desert and mountain in quest of treasure.

Many years ago, clamming along the Mississippi and other Midwestern rivers was a thriving business—synthetics hadn't yet replaced the pearl button, made from the shells. Itinerant wraiths of women in gingham and overalled men roamed from river to river, searching for the big pearl, but settling mainly for seed pearls, which were sold for ornamenting jewelry. They earned just about enough to keep them in bread and whiskey. And though they never quite reached it, they were trying for the rainbow.

In the beginning, I knew nothing of pearls, nothing of the people who hunted them. Then one night, having gone to my cot, I heard a strange sound and, lifting to an elbow so I could look through the window screen, I saw flashlight beams crisscrossing the glade. Next morning there was a tent, and I discovered that one woman and two men had moved in during the night, though for what—since they had no fish poles—I couldn't imagine. I stayed my distance all day and waited until that night to ask my father what they might be doing.

"Likely looking for pearls," he said.

Pearls! In my Rock River! I didn't sleep much that night. The next morning, I threaded my duck skiff along their trail, putting out cane fish poles so they wouldn't know I was spying. The men waded chest-deep in the river, feeling for the clams with their feet, and dunking at intervals to bring them up. When they had a boatload, they rowed to shore and began to open them and search for pearls.

I stowed my poles and hastened around a bend so I'd be out of sight. Then I began collecting clams. When I had a black mound of them, I paddled back to our cottage, got a knife, and sat down to open them. The harder I tried, the tighter the clams closed their shells. I tried smashing them between two rocks. They broke open, but the flesh was crushed and juice spattered on my bare legs. I scraped and bruised and cut my fingers, but I found no pearls.

The men had had no difficulty in opening the clams, so when they were once again hunched over a mound of black shells, I crept through the grass to where I could watch. It was instantly clear that the knives they were using were thrust to a point just above the hinge and then rocked back and forth. I backed away and returned to my own pile of clams. Now, when I hit the muscle, the clam relaxed and I could pry the shells apart. Then I went carefully through the meat.

I went for days without finding a pearl. Finally, when the men were out on the river, I found enough courage to approach the woman, who stayed in the camp and did the cooking. She was fat and wore a man's shoes with no socks, and though I didn't get close, I could smell moonshine. She was sitting on a stump drinking coffee from a tin cup, and for a while she just looked at me. I was about to turn and run when she said, "Yes, boy?"

It was a strangely wonderful voice, deep and throaty. It stopped me in my tracks. Although she had spoken but two words, it came to me at once that she was lonely and sad. I stared a long time before I realized I was staring. Then, to cover up, I said, "Could I ask you some questions?"

She laughed a little, and the sound of her laughter was as soothing as the sound of her voice. She replied, "I guess so, because I don't have to answer them if I don't want to."

So I explained that I wanted to learn how to find pearls, that I knew about getting the shells open, but that I didn't know how to go through the clam meat without dumping it into a pail and fingering through it.

She got up and went to a pile of empty clamshells. A cyclone of flies lifted as she bent to get one. Then she came back and told me to watch while she ran her thumbs along each side of the shell under the meat to the spots where the pearls—if there were any—usually lay. She explained that you had to feel the pearls rather than see them, and that it was even good to shut your eyes while thumbing along beneath the meat so as to be able to concentrate on the sense of touch.

"When you feel one, you'll know it," she said. "Get it between your thumb and forefinger, and put it up under your upper lip. When you've sucked it clean, spit it into a small bottle."

Then she was silent. After a time, I dared to look into her face and ask, "Is that all there is to it?"

She gave her tin cup a toss, and coffee grounds went spraying into a clump of cattails. She looked into the bottom of the cup as though there might be a pearl in it, and said, "That's all. That's all that you'd understand." She got up heavily and sighed.

"Thank you," I said, turning away.

Out of the corner of my eye I saw her turn toward me
again. She put a hand to her face and said quietly, "Don't

thank me, boy. It's no life, believe me. Forget the pearls. You'll starve trying."

The next day I felt the first nubbin beneath my thumb and brought my first seed pearl to light. It was almost as big as a perch's eye, and though it wasn't completely round, its color took my breath away. I quickly put it into my mouth, sucked it clean, and then, holding a small medicine bottle to my lips, spat the pearl into it. It shone like captured sunshine. I found two small ones that day. Even my family was excited by my discovery. We sat around the kerosene lamp until way past my bedtime, admiring and talking about the pearls.

After that there was no time for anything else. Buck, my dog, had a droopy, sad look in his eye because I had no time to hunt and swim with him, and the fishermen who saw me feeling for clams with my feet asked what that crazy kid was up to. There were circles under my eyes because I got up so early and was still opening clams long after the mosquitoes had claimed the night as their own.

But when I got back into shoes to go to school, I had a small wineglass full of the most beautiful pearls a man could ever want to see. None was round enough to be worth much. I knew that, but it made no difference, because I didn't want to sell them anyway.

Then came the day when I went next door to show the pearls to my grandmother's new boarder. I had spread them on the card table, when Buck came running through the room and upset the table. All the pearls went down the large, circular hot-air register of my grandmother's furnace.

I nearly died. And sometimes I think a tiny part of me did. I braved the searing heat and went through the dust and grime which had been accumulating in the old furnace for years, but I never found one of my precious pearls. I figured I had wasted my entire summer.

But now that I look back, I know that the summer wasn't

wasted. Now I know that the real value was not in the pearls but in the dream. I have never dreamed so grandly since; and, in all the years between, I have never come to any adventure with such a singleness of purpose. In losing the pearls, I learned the hardest lesson: All life is transient; only dreams endure.

Mel Ellis

SEASON OF THE EMPTY NEST

Remember when the children built blanket tents to sleep in? And then scrambled by moonlight to their own beds, where they'd be safe from bears? And how proud and eager they were to be starting kindergarten? But only up to the minute they got there? And the time they packed cardboard suitcases in such a huff? "You won't see *us* again!" they hollered. Then they turned back at the end of the yard because they'd forgotten to go to the bathroom.

It's the same thing when they're 20 or 22, starting to make their own way in the grownup world. Bravado, pangs, false starts and pratfalls. They're half in, half out. "Good-by, good-by! Don't worry, Mom!" They're back the first weekend to borrow the paint roller and a fuse and a broom. Prowling the attic, they seize on the quilt the dog ate and the terrible old sofa cushions that smell like dead mice. "Just what I need!" they cheer, loading the car.

"Good-by, good-by!" implying forever. But they show up without notice at suppertimes, sighing soulfully to see the familiar laden plates. They go away again, further secured by four bags of groceries, the electric frying pan and a cookbook.

They call home collect, but not as often as parents need to hear. And their news makes fast-graying hair stand on end: "...so he forgot to set the brake, and he says my car rolled three blocks backward down the hill before it was totaled!" "...simple case of last hired, first fired, no big deal. I sold the stereo, and..." "Mom! Everybody in the city has them! There's this roach stuff you put under the sink. It's..."

I gripped the phone with both hands in those days, wishing I could bribe my children back with everything they'd ever wanted—drum lessons, a junk-food charge account, anything. I struggled with an unbecoming urge to tell them once more about hot breakfasts and crossing streets and dry socks on wet days.

"I'm *so* impressed by how you cope!" I said instead.

The children scatter, and parents draw together, remembering sweet-shaped infants heavy in their arms, patched jeans, chicken pox, the night the accident happened, the rituals of Christmases and proms. With wistful pride and a feeling for the comic, they watch over their progeny from an effortfully kept distance. It is the season of the empty nest.

Slowly, slowly, there are changes. Something wonderful seems to hover then, faintly heard, glimpsed in illumined moments. Visiting the children, the parents are almost sure of it.

A son spreads a towel on the table and efficiently irons a perfect crease into his best pants. (*Ironing board*, his mother thinks, adding to a mental shopping list.) "I'm taking you to a French restaurant for dinner," the young man announces. "I've made reservations."

"Am I properly dressed?" his mother asks, suddenly shy. He walks her through city streets within the aura of his assurance. His arm lies lightly around her shoulders.

Or a daughter offers her honored guests the only two chairs she has and settles into a harem heap of floor pillows. She has raised plants from cuttings, framed a wall full of prints herself, spent three weekends refinishing the little dresser that glows in a square of sun.

Her parents regard her with astonished love. The room has been enchanted by her touch. "Everything's charming," they tell her honestly. "It's a real home."

Now? Is it *now*? Yes. The something wonderful descends. The generations smile at one another, as if exchanging congratulations. The children are no longer children. The parents are awed to discover adults.

It is wonderful, in ways my imagination had not begun to dream on. How could I have guessed—how could they?— that of my three, the shy one would pluck a dazzling array of competencies out of the air and turn up, chatting with total poise, on TV shows? That the one who turned his adolescence into World War III would find his role in arduous, sensitive human service? Or that the unbookish, antic one, torment of his teachers, would evolve into a scholar, tolerating a student's poverty and writing into the night?

I hadn't suspected that my own young adults would be so ebulliently funny one minute, and so tellingly introspective the next; so open-hearted and unguarded. Or that growing up would inspire them to buy life insurance and three-piece suits and lend money to the siblings they'd once robbed of lollypops. Or that walking into their houses, I'd hear Mozart on the tape player and find books laid out for me to borrow.

Once, long ago, I waited nine months at a time to see who they would be, babes newly formed and wondrous. "Oh, *look!*" I said, and fell in love. Now my children are wondrously new to me in a different way. I am in love again.

My daughter and I freely share the complex world of our inner selves, and all the other worlds we know. Touched, I notice how her rhythms and gestures are reminding of her grandmother's or mine. We are linked by unconscious mysteries and benignly watched by ghosts. I turn my head to gaze at her. She meets my look and smiles.

A son flies the width of the country for his one vacation in a whole long year. He follows me around the kitchen, tasting from the pots, handing down the dishes. We brown in the sun. Read books in silent synchrony. He jogs. I tend the flowers. We walk at the unfurled edge of great waves. We talk and talk, and later play cribbage past midnight. I'm utterly happy.

"But, it's your vacation!" I remind him. "What shall we do that's special?"

"This," he says. "Exactly this."

When my children first ventured out and away, I felt they were in flight to outer space, following a curve of light and time to such unknowns that my heart would surely go faint with trying to follow. I thought this would be the end of parenting. Not what it is—the best part; the final, firmest bonding; the goal and the reward.

Joan Mills

The point at which your child becomes an adult is a marvelous and miraculous thing. One day you are battling over everything, you feel the scornful lift of the eyelid, the dreadful arrogance of adolescence. Suddenly it changes. You find yourself at ease, talking together as two who have a basic love for each other. The stress and strain are gone, there is comradeship, new and strange and fine. It is an experience as lovely as the first white tulip in the spring.

Gladys Taber and
Barbara Webster

In his autobiography written in 1981, a year before his death, film star Henry Fonda shared an early memory:

When I was five, my mother woke me up and took me to the window and showed me Halley's comet streaking across the sky. She told me to remember it always, because, she said, it comes around only once every 76 years, and 76 years is a long time.

Well, that's how old I am now—The years seem to have gone by as fast as Halley's comet. But I don't think of myself as old. I still think of myself as the boy on the landing looking out of the window.

Henry Fonda

SEASONS OF JOY

HURRAY! IT'S RAINING!

We had spent several weeks in southern Spain, at the hottest time of the year. Early every morning my young son went to the balcony of our hotel to see what kind of day it would be, and every day it was the same—inexhaustibly sunny—until one morning I heard a whoop of joy and the exultant words, "Hurray! It's raining!"

Glorious to see the dusty streets and rooftops running with rain! Delightful to breathe the cleansed air, to smell the wet earth! Through the whole of that streaming day, Longfellow's poem sang in my mind:

How beautiful is the rain!
After the dust and heat,
In the broad and fiery street,
In the narrow lane,
How beautiful is the rain!

Rain is always marvelous, and always brings with it special sights and sounds and feelings. When I was a small girl, I had a fussy nursemaid who never allowed me to go out in what she called "weather." How wistfully I watched, from my window, processions of drenched and gleaming children passing by on rainy days— shining in slickers, belted and booted, wet, windblown, red-cheeked. Their condition seemed altogether idyllic.

Then one summer I was sent to visit my aunt in the country. I had never been there before, and I was wildly excited. A city child, I longed to make friends with a tree or a rock. But on my first morning in the big house, I awakened to a sound that filled me with dismay: rain, running on the roof and gurgling in the gutters; rain, streaming down the giant elms, rapping at the windows. I supposed I would have to spend the day indoors, fretful and forlorn.

I could have wept. With all my heart, I had looked forward to exploring the woods behind the house. My long face must have shown my disappointment, for Aunt Alice asked what was wrong. When I told her, she said briskly, "Stay *in* because of the rain? Nonsense! Come on, I want to show you something."

Incredibly, she led me right out the door. "We'll leave our shoes on the stoop," she said, taking hers off matter-of-factly. Laughing all the way, we ran like a pair of dryads over the grass, into the woods and along the ferned and mossy banks of a brook. Deeper and deeper we traveled into an enchanted forest of dripping trees and grasses, until we came to a little dell, half-screened by foliage.

Thrusting the screening branches aside, Aunt Alice commanded, "Look!"

The dell was thickly carpeted with mushrooms—thousands of them, it seemed to me. I caught my breath. "Are they *really* mushrooms?" I asked.

"They're *really* umbrellas for elves," Aunt Alice replied.

It was the perfect answer, and I have been a rain lover ever since.

Rain offers infinite variety of mood. Sometimes there is a restful monotony about continued wet weather. One tends to sleep a lot, to store energy. Hours melt away in rivulets, 54 almost unnoticed. At other times, rain gives us a sense of uncertainty, deepening before a thunderstorm to a positive suspense; we almost brace for the thunder. And I like this, the uncertainty and suspense, the *relationship* with the weather.

There is a special bond of pride and pleasure between people who like to walk in the rain. Whenever I see a boy and girl walking together on wet days, holding hands, I remember a certain blind date of my youth. The boy's parents were friends of my parents. We were wary and hideously polite until we emerged from our New York restaurant into rain. The boy started to call a taxi. "But I love to walk in the rain," I burst out.

"Why," his face lighted up, "so do I!"

We gazed at each other in pleased discovery. Amazing coincidence, instant kinship. Freedom and adventure seized us, and we set forth, noisily exuberant, for Times Square, a mile away.

There beauty silenced us. It was September, and the rain was very fine, mixed with fog, that luminous sort of rain that catches the light and builds a city of illusion. We stood quietly, surrounded by enormous neon signs, their blinking lights no longer garish, but softened by a million tiny droplets of moisture, magnified and reflected by the glistening streets.

Breaking into our reverie, a stranger asked, "Pardon me, but is this Times Square?" We nodded. But, of course, it was not; it was Times Square in a misting September rain. And that is altogether different.

I have seen even greater transformations wrought by rain. On a family automobile trip one winter, we stopped for the night as a cold drizzle began to fall. The motel was in a dreary little town, with nothing to interest the children. We were so tired that the trip seemed something of a mistake.

We fell heavily asleep. I awakened first, hearing a clacking sound outside the window. I drew the blind—and involuntarily exclaimed, "Oh!" Outside, sparkling in the sun of the new day, a grove of trees looked as though it had been fashioned of glass, of diamond, of a precious spun-silver material. The frozen rain had changed a cheerless town into a fantastic wonderland.

Hastily my husband and I awakened the children, hustled them into their clothes, rushed them out of doors! We took pictures, tasted icicles — and blessed the night showers that had given us this morning.

How beautiful is the rain. The clouds lower. A pattering begins. There is — yes, there is — a drop upon the pane, and another. And now a celebration of them, a torrent.

Hurray! It's raining!

Elizabeth Starr Hill

RICHES

I know where wild forget-me-nots wade
Along the edge of clear running water —
Where a great blue heron stands at sunrise.
I have listened to the first spring peepers
and have counted the varied and tender
greens of spring, from pale of willow
to dark of pine.
I have walked on pine-needle carpets
and on spongy green moss
In sunlight and shade —
I know a woodland pool
hidden from sight
by giant ferns,

Where mayapples
unfurl their green umbrellas
beneath a stone lantern
and the small face of the hepatica
holds a drop of blue sky.

I have uncovered
the damp sweetness of arbutus,
and felt the south wind
brush across my face
bearing a hint of rain
and flower gardens.

I have seen the scarlet tanager
in the topmost branches
of the tulip tree,
and the marsh wren in her house
beneath the lemon lilies.
I know a pond at evening
Where ducks trail silver threads
in their wake, trout jump,
and fireflies appear above the water.

I have seen the whippoorwill
silhouetted on a dusky sky
and heard his song
of summer magic—
And standing in bright moonlight
Watching shadows cast by giant pines
I have felt the mystery of heaven
and the joy of earth—
and I know what I know—
These are the things to remember.

Katharine G. Shelly

"TELL US HOW TO BE HAPPY"

When a group of children in the Boston slums confronted Alice Freeman Palmer with: "Tell us how to be happy," she asked them to try to look for something pretty every day for a week. "Don't skip a day," she cautioned, "or it won't work. A leaf, a flower, a cloud—you can all find something. And stop long enough to see the loveliness all through." At the end of the week, Mrs. Palmer met one of the girls out walking her baby brother. "I done it!" the youngster told Mrs. Palmer triumphantly. "I never skipped a day, neither, and it was awful hard. It was all right when I could go to the park, but one day it rained and the baby had a cold, and I just couldn't go out. I thought sure I was going to skip, and I was standin' at the window, 'most cryin', and I saw—I saw a sparrow taking a bath in the gutter that goes round the top of the house, and he had on a black necktie, and he was handsome. And then there was another day, the baby was sick, and I saw his hair. A little bit of sun came in the window, and I saw his hair." She thrust the baby toward Mrs. Palmer, and the sun playing on its hair picked up the browns, the reds and the golds of Titian hair. "See, isn't it beautiful?" the child asked. "Now I'll never be lonesome again."

George Herbert Palmer

JOY AND PAIN

To live fully, we must experience both.

My husband and I recently saw a play about an elderly couple spending their 44th summer in Maine. The underlying theme was their sense of time running out, of their own mortality. We were deeply moved by the old couple. We laughed at their charming eccentricities and wept at their anguish. As the play ended, a woman in front of us said loudly to her companion, "I *can't stand* plays that try to make me cry!"

I felt sorry for that woman. If she could not bear to look at the dying, she must not have noticed the loving and the living, which were present in equal part.

It is possible to skim the surface of life without being profoundly touched by anything, but it's not very rewarding. Those who close themselves off from pain must also sacrifice opportunities to feel a piercing sense of joy. To feel deeply, to know the fullest dimensions of ourselves and others, we must feel *everything*.

I know a woman whose only daughter died at age 35, leaving two young children. The grandmother lives in New York, the two granddaughters in Alaska. Friends urged Grandma to visit her grandchildren after their mother's death. "No, I can't," she said. "Jenny looks just the way Helen did as a child; it would kill me to see her."

Ten years later, when Jenny was 18, she wrote that she was coming to New York. Her grandmother replied that she was sorry, but it was an inconvenient time for a visit — her apartment was about to be painted.

Helen had been my friend, so I invited Jenny to visit me. When she walked through the door, I began to cry. It *was* shocking to see an almost perfect replica of Helen. I could understand how painful such a sight would be for Helen's mother. But in avoiding that pain, she also cheated herself of the pleasure I had reliving some of the happy times I'd had with Helen. Jenny's visit reminded me of the loss, but I also felt a sense of thanksgiving—even triumph—that so much of Helen lived on in Jenny. I cried and won; Grandma ran away and lost.

It seems to me that the capacity for finding joy in the most ordinary events (watching a flower open, leaves turning red, a bird taking a bath) deepens each time I live through great sorrow. Death makes life more precious; frustration makes success more fulfilling.

The capacity to feel is an especially crucial issue for parents. Our natural inclination is to try to protect children from pain. We think that if a child is happy we are doing a good job; if a child is sad we are failing as parents. But giving children the message that happy is good and sad is terrible decreases their capacity to explore the full range of human experiences.

Children need to understand that suffering, frustration and failure are not only inevitable but helpful. Such experiences can help develop the patience, persistence and ability to cope that they'll need when a scientific experiment fails, a low grade is received after diligent study, or a belly flop occurs after a summer of diving lessons. There is nothing so terrible about failing and feeling pain; what hurts in the long run is not trying because of the fear of pain.

This is particularly true of human relationships. I once heard a father tell his nine-year-old son: "It doesn't matter if David won't play with you anymore; he wasn't a nice person anyway." But the breakup of a friendship always hurts. If we push it aside we diminish the meaning—and much of the joy—of such relationships.

The stiff-upper-lip approach can cripple a child's capacity to feel. If we say, for example, "Stop whining about David; act like a man and take your lumps," the child may withdraw from his feelings because he is too lonely with them. It would be more helpful to say, "I know how you feel. It hurts when a good friend deserts you, and it takes a while to start feeling better."

In allowing pain into our lives, we need to strike a balance between puritanically "facing reality" and the other extreme of evasion. My husband once gave me a saying that I posted above my desk: *The only thing I fear is that I will not be worthy of my own suffering.* Every time I feel miserable, hopeless or anxious, I read that statement. It's a continuing reminder that if I *am* worthy of my own suffering—if I allow it and use it to increase my self-knowledge and my compassion for others—I'll also be worthy of the moments of joy that will inevitably follow.

Eda LeShan

*There's so much spectating going on
that a lot of us never get around to living.
Life is always walking up to us
and saying, "Come on in, the living's fine."
And what do we do?
Back off and take its picture.*

Russell Baker

HYACINTHS TO FEED THE SOUL

An unexpected gift, a small extravagance can give life a lift when it's needed most.

When I was a student nurse, I baby-sat during off-duty hours to help pay my way. One day I got a call to sit for a whole weekend.

All I knew when I headed for the job was that the couple wanted to "get away" from their two kids for a few days. Expecting that only rich people would be able to do that, I was surprised when the address turned out to be a tiny house in the borderline part of the city.

Ted, the husband, had just joined an architectural firm. His wife, Ardeth, looked terribly tired. They waited, obviously anxious to be off, while I got acquainted with the children, 2½ years and 11 months old. I held the baby against my shoulder while Ted gave me the name of their hotel. "You'll be there the whole time?" I asked.

"That's headquarters," Ted answered. "We'll sleep late, prowl around town, eat when we get hungry, visit the art galleries..."

Mentally, I added up the cost of all that, plus my fee— ten dollars. "But won't that be terribly expensive?" I blurted. I had adopted them already.

"Why, yes, I guess it will," Ted said. "But it's important. We're both tired and snapping at each other. Ardeth, especially, needs to get away from the children."

Ardeth smiled at me. "Don't you know about hyacinths to feed the soul?" She took a volume from the bookcase and opened it to a poem by someone called the Gulistan of Moslih Eddin Saadi, a sheik who lived more than 700 years ago:

If of thy mortal goods thou art bereft,

And from thy slender store two loaves alone to
  thee are left,
Sell one, and with the dole
Buy hyacinths to feed thy soul.

That poem taught me a good deal. Those two didn't have enough money for the trip, but they were tuned in on a set of values I'd never even thought of. Sunday night, when they came back, they looked like teenagers who'd just discovered love. And my ten dollars was tucked under the ribbon on a pot holding a lavender hyacinth.

Over the years since, I've made a hobby of noticing people and whether or not they know about using nonessentials and extravagances occasionally to feed the soul. The happiest people do.

A church organist I know grew up in a farm family during the Depression. They did not starve, but her childhood was not happy. "Then, when I was in seventh grade, things changed," she told me. "My folks bought a secondhand piano, and arranged with a music teacher in town to accept vegetables in payment for my lessons. The neighbors called it a useless extravagance. The miracle is that my folks knew what was important. Twenty cashmere sweaters couldn't have charged me with the confidence that piano gave me."

A no-nonsense mother I know lets Christmas and family birthdays release her usual tight lid on frivolity. "When I was a child," she explains, "gifts were always sturdy shoes, warm gloves, underwear. After I got married, I decided that we'd somehow manage the essentials, that the special occasions would be for fun. Now my husband and I give each other and the kids wild things we'd never dare include in the budget." Her idea of zingy gifts: tickets to a far-out play, a white-velvet coat she has worn twice and had cleaned twice but which makes her feel positively elegant; for the children, redeemable coupons for gooey treats at the ice-cream store.

Flowers given on birthdays or other predictable occasions are hardly hyacinths. But when bouquets are offered to celebrate Monday, or "the anniversary of the day we got the car paid for," or simply as "thank you for putting up with me so long"—what a different matter!

To send a relative a card on his birthday is not unusual. But to pop a note into the mail, apropos of nothing, is a hyacinth. The mother who spells "I love you" with chocolate chips on top of the no-occasion cake is proclaiming loud and clear that she *cares*.

When our stomachs are empty, we get hungry. Symptoms of soul starvation are subtler. Tomorrows and tomorrows are rolling by. Paychecks are being spent on bread and shoes and rent, while the walls of our souls remain bare. If this matters to us, we can do something: we can buy hyacinths.

Carol Amen

Peace is not a season;
it is a way of life.

Abbey Press

JOY ALONG THE WAY

A summer visit to Aunt Marg was no mere vacation, but a journey into a world of enchantment.

Aunt Marg lived at the foot of Buzzard's Roost Mountain in Mill Creek, Missouri, in an ancient house wreathed by dense quince bushes and bracketed by cedars. The last quarter mile leading to the house was a graveled creek bed. Aunt Marg considered this natural road a bountiful gift. If there was water in the creek, so much the better. It washed the buggy wheels.

During summer, Mama allowed my sisters and me, one at a time, to go stay a week with Aunt Marg. The visit was to help her out some, for, as everyone agreed, Aunt Marg had a lot to do. Yet the phrase "to help her out some" was said as if there might be more to it.

When, at age nine, I came down the rickety, narrow stairway on the morning of my first visit, Aunt Marg greeted me with, "Oh, I've got the busiest day today!"

"What do you have to do?" I asked shyly, for Aunt Marg was new to me and I didn't know what to expect. She was tall and bony, her face a network of fine creases.

"I've got to take the wind chimes to the top of Buzzard's Roost," she told me.

"I'll help," I said, wondering what wind chimes were and why they had to be taken up Buzzard's Roost.

I thought we'd get started right after breakfast, but first there was the cow to be milked. Then there were the chickens to feed—silver-laced Wyandottes. "Not the best layers," Aunt Marg said. "But see here." She picked up a gray feather from the chicken yard and pointed out the silver scalloped lining. "Now that's *something*," she said.

As the day wore on, I wondered why Aunt Marg hadn't
said, "I've got to work in the garden" instead of "I've got

to take the wind chimes to the top of Buzzard's Roost." Gardening seemed the major chore of the now hot and sticky day. But finally, in midafternoon, she went upstairs and came back with a box tied with twine. It rattled like broken glass.

Even then we didn't go straight up the mountain but zig—zaggy. There were many things for Aunt Marg to check on.

"Now right over there ought to be my sheep." Aunt Marg pointed through thick brush and trees to a little clearing.

"I didn't know you had sheep," I ventured.

"Oh no, child. They're really Rash Bannister's. But I call 'em mine," she chuckled.

In the clearing were a dozen or so sheep and one lamb. They came to meet us. Though they all looked alike to me, they took turns nuzzling Aunt Marg's hand when she called each one by name.

Leaving them in the mountainside meadow, we resumed the climb. Suddenly Aunt Marg stopped. "Wild roses," she said. I looked around and couldn't see any. "They'll be right over there." She pointed a finger and, even before they came into view, I began to smell their fresh spiciness.

At a rocky outcropping, Aunt Marg stopped again. "Isn't it just wonderful!" she exclaimed. But all I could see was valley below. From this height the spring creek looked like a silver ribbon rippling across the cow pasture. Thin blue woodsmoke arose from invisible chimneys in the folds of the hills. A wagonload of hay creaked along the graveled road.

On, up and up we went until we reached the tip-top of Buzzard's Roost. "Just wonderful!" Aunt Marg breathed once again. She waved her hands in a circle to indicate the whole visible world. Then she sat down, untied the package and took out the wind chimes.

"I made 'em myself," she said, rather proudly. There were little circular bands of hickory, looking very much like embroidery hoops. From them, dangling on different lengths of string, were glued–on pieces of broken glass. Even as she took them from the box and began to sort them out, I could hear the fairy–like music they made as they brushed against one another. Then Aunt Marg attached the wind chimes to the branch of a pine tree.

Capricious breezes gently tossed the pine and spun a spell of magic. The thin, clear music of the chimes began to reach something inside of me that had not been touched before. After a while it utterly possessed me, calling up a merry bub-bling so strong and compelling that I seemed to be dangling from some unseen string myself—light, helpless with hap-piness, yet in the firm grasp of some sustaining power.

Soon the sheep had come up the mountain, maybe called by the wind chimes, to lie by us. The lamb was close to me. I put out my hand, and it jumped up and leaped over clumps of mullen, twisting in mid–air and coming down stiff-legged as if putting into action all the enchantment of the mountaintop. Mentally, I named the lamb "Wind Chimes," then told Aunt Marg of my naming.

She said she'd speak to Rash about it. "But, of course, they're ours, too, you know," she reminded. She looked at me skeptically as if I were too young to understand, but I think I did. I had seen the lamb's fancy frolic and felt the warm sunshine on its fresh new fleece. I sensed the in-nocence, the suggestion that all things should leap for joy. Indeed, the whole world seemed mine alone.

Aunt Marg carefully took down the chimes, put them into the box and we started down the mountain.

When I returned home, my sisters asked if I'd helped Aunt Marg, and I nodded silently, unable then to put into words what the visit had meant.

But I know now that Aunt Marg held up before us, in her own uncomplicated way, the uncommonness of the com-mon. By stating that she had to do pleasurable things, she implied that this was our duty also. She taught us always to keep something to look forward to, to let it "embroider" our thought as we go about the business of living. Most of all, she taught us that when we see some little frills like mountainside wild roses or a chicken feather's scalloped lining to stop and wonder if they aren't put there for our delight, to provide joy along the way.

Jean Bell Mosley

Climb the mountains and get their good tidings.
Nature's peace will flow into you
as sunshine flows into trees. The winds
will blow their freshness into you,
and the storms their energy,
while cares will drop off like falling leaves.

John Muir

THE RARITY OF JUNE

The slat of sunshine surprises the dust on the chair — and I am suddenly back in the slant-roofed bedroom, to which the wind and the rain gave an added snugness.

I run to the window and look out. It is a shadowless day in June. The cows, great bulks of contentment, are grazing near the bars of the zigzag pasture fence. Their sides are covered with outlines of Tasmania and Zanzibar where the patches of white hair alternate with the brown. This fascinates me. What mapmaker beneath the skin can cause the hair to grow white and then, once across the irregular but precise edge of the patches, to grow brown?

As if at a signal, the scattered cows stop their grazing. They wind in single file back up the cow path between the alders to sprawl motionless in the shade of the two giant maples that stand at the crest of the blueberry slope. The cows' huge liquid eyes squint tight, then open wide, with the rhythms and logarithms of safety and peace.

Nearer the house, the wild-crabapple tree foams with blossoms and bees intent as theologians. Its branches patiently scrawl the lesson of universal branching on the stainless air. The blue half-shell of a robin's egg lies on the ground beneath it, like a tiny fallen sky. Swallows, with a bit of glistening mud or a hyphen of straw in their beaks and a murmur in their throats akin to deliciously soft-edged "x's" tumbling together, swoop toward their purse-mouthed houses, building under every eave.

Sounds do not disturb this day. The rushing of the brook, the cowbells, voices in another field — none of them roams out to claim the ear as on other days; they are content where they are. Each object and all its inflections — the slope of a hill, the curve of the road, the up-and-downness of trees, the back-and-forthness of weatherboarding on the house — bask in being exactly themselves. A flock of crows, their wariness and their portent suspended, configure nothing but crow flight above the drowsing churchyard.

The air smells of sunlight and grass. Of towels on the line and the clean angles of gable roofs. Of warm-rock breath and the cloth over rising bread. Of tree sap and leaf spine. Of wild roses on the stone wall and milk cans hanging in the well. Of the imminence of apples and the hair of children....

We are planting. The ground has been ribboned into dark-brown furrows. They lie like brothers side by side, the earth's rich secrets exposed willingly to the sun.

The horse grazes in harness at the edge of the field while my father cuts the seed potatoes. He studies each potato for a moment, then with a surgeon's skill slices it into sections that will each have two eyes. My mother goes up and down the rows, drawing a light chain behind her to smooth the seedbed. A neighbor notices this. He is himself full of the strange amity of planting time.

"Joe," he calls across to my father, "did you know that Mary was loose?"

We all laugh.

I think: *Isn't it wonderful that he'll be living next to us all our lives!* And I think: *If we get our potatoes sown first, why don't we go over and give him a hand with his?*

I picture how it will go. When he sees us coming with our baskets he'll know we're coming to help, but he'll pretend we're just coming to talk.

"Does it matter which of these bags we take the seed out of?" Father will say.

"No," he says then, "not a particle. But now you fellows don't have to..."

He knows we will, though. And when we do, won't there be a tingling fellowship among us!

I walk along the rows my mother has chained. I drop the seed almost sedately, to make sure the spacing never varies. It is as if with each seed I am marking off another interval of pure balm in this humming day. My body rejoices: its 70 own total inspiration.

My mother's face wears itself gently and becomingly, and my father is stronger than anyone I know. She moves up close to him to ask about the "small seeds." She always sows the small seeds. They make no special sign of intimacy, but all at once something about their nearness fills up that little hollow in the perfect day put there by the day's very perfection.

I watch and I marvel. Seed potatoes are no mystery: they just grow more potatoes like themselves. But how are the plumpness and the redness of the grown beet contained in that tiny brown burr? The greeness and the warts of the cucumber in that tiny white eye lens? The cone and the tartness of the parsnip in that little oatmeal wafer? The cheek-flesh of the turnip and the leaf-pack of the cabbage in those miniature purple spheres so alike that you couldn't tell which was turnip seed and which cabbage unless they were marked?

She covers the seeds with just a sprinkling of sifted earth and pats it down. I look at her hands...and I look at my father's hands as they guide the handles of the plow so skillfully that the wave of earth the plow tumbles onto the potatoes covers each of them to exactly the same depth...and from every detail of everything I look at comes the sudden exclamation of its falling exultantly into place with me.

Ernest Buckler

A WHISKER OF PRIDE

All summer she had waited for this moment. Now it was time to reach into the unknown.

Growing up is a discarding of dreams—the not-to-be triumphs, the too-dizzying heights, the still-distant horizons. They come in the golden rush of childhood, but they cannot stay. They won't telescope down to the ordinary strictures of time laid out for the chores that need doing.

Yet sometimes, in the long years of burdens, there's a madcap, will-o'-the-wisp moment when—like a child—we can grab at a sparkle in the sky. Reach high for such moments; don't let them pass. For once they are gone they may not come again, and we will have missed a brightness.

All summer I had waited for such a chance, a tiny dream teasing in my mind. Finally it came.

A mile and a half across from our vacation place on Parry Island in Ontario's Georgian Bay lies Palestine Island, a long, dark slope of rock slabs and pine trees. In the evening the sun sets beyond Palestine in a running fire of gold and rose, and then, through a crook in the trees, the distant Carling Rock Lighthouse shines down the night like a blue star.

On a Palestine cliff in a straight line across from our beach is a white house, looking small as a cardboard toy, surrounded by shadows. Only rarely does some unseen hand light a lamp so the windows gleam as if a spark of sun had caught in the glass. I had been watching that house over the years; now, suddenly, a desire arose in me—without rhyme or reason, utterly inappropriate—to swim the dark waters to its isolation.

But of course it was ridiculous. I am a grandmother. I have five children. In the world's eye I have done nothing all these years but housework, and we all know *that* is not conducive to the body beautiful. Although I had come to love swimming, and each summer vacation tried painfully to teach myself the art, it really hadn't worked. Once, when someone told me I was swimming in 20 feet of water, I almost drowned from sudden hysteria.

But that tiny dream kept buzzing through my thoughts. So I began to practice regularly—until "Mother's daily dip" became a family joke. I never missed a day, even in storms, sometimes emerging almost strangled from the banging waves. All the time I was waiting—waiting for strength, for confidence, for a calm day not too cold, and for a scarcity of folks to argue me out of it.

The summer passed without those conditions. Wistfully, I gave up the dream, telling myself I was really too old anyway. Then, late on the last afternoon of vacation, when I was standing on the shore looking out over the water toward the distant, brooding house, the moment came.

The bay was empty of boats since most of the cottagers had already departed. All my family had left, too, save my youngest son. When I dipped my foot in the water, I was surprised it was no colder. The wind of the last two days had died, and the waves were rolling in, easy and gentle. Across the bay the sinking sun was laying a path of gold to my feet, inviting me, urging me, and suddenly, in a lonely calmness, I knew this was my chance into the unknown of what I could do.

I ran back to the cabin where my son was practicing his guitar and rapped on the window.

"I'm swimming to Palestine," I said.

A chord broke off in midair. "Are you crazy?"

"No, serious. Get the canoe, lifejackets, a coat and towel. I've got to hurry. There's only about an hour of daylight left."

I whirled back to the shore and eased into the gold path of sunlight. I swam carefully, testing myself. My muscles felt supple and sure and I breathed easier.

The sun was skidding into the horizon, dimming my path, when my son, bewildered, paddled up and asked if I was all right.

"Fine," I said, meaning my head included, and swam on, at intervals varying my strokes from breast to back to left and right side.

The darkening distance ahead seemed to stretch implacably, and then the sun went down completely and my path disappeared in the black waters. I had not realized how the cold of the deeper water would eat into my marrow. A layer of numbness ringed my body, and doubts began to arise. *Could* I finish? Should I keep trying? Was I being foolish?

My son asked me urgently, "Are you cold?"

"No!" A firm lie.

"Are you tired?"

"No!" Another lie.

"Don't you want to turn back?"

"No!" The truth this time.

I swam on, counting strokes, watching for my son's paddle when he pointed it, showing how I was off course. Then I would straighten my line, doggedly trying not to cough or choke, though once a spray of unexpected wake caught me wrong. I no longer looked toward the white house. It stayed too far away, fading into a glimmer shrouded by night.

On and on, and then a little roughness of water and I realized I was in the main channel. I almost laughed. I must be getting there. Overhead the stars were coming out and I watched a scrap of twinkling as though it were a bird leading me on.

Another hundred backstrokes and suddenly I slid into warm, quiet water. I turned over and looked up, and the white house was above my head, a silent, watching presence. Almost languidly I breaststroked into that view, closer and closer. My foot felt the hard cliff shelving under the water and I stood up, and my son was laughing, wrapping my head in his shirt, drying me with a towel, saying over and over,

"What a wild, crazy mother you are."

And oh! I was proud. I had swum to Palestine!

Well, of course, the world with a great whoosh flipflopped me from the black rock of Palestine back to my winter kitchen and my winter chores of dinner by the clock, proper clothes with functioning zippers and accurate laundering. And that moment of shining pride faded and dwindled until only a whisker remained. And one morning, doing dishes, I wondered if I would forget entirely.

Then, through the window, I saw on my lawn a cobweb from the night—an old lady's cap, we used to call it. And dew hung on it—sparkling drops laced in sunlight like jewels . . . like jewels dropped from a wind off . . . off Palestine, of course! I smiled in my mind, for I knew then there would be no forgetting. That whisker of pride was mine forever.

Mary Roelofs Stott

You can't take a crash course in serenity.

Shirley MacLaine

Charles Lindbergh's description of the end of his 1927 solo flight across the Atlantic:

Within the hour I'll land, and strangely enough I'm in no hurry to have it pass. I haven't the slightest desire to sleep. There's not an ache in my body. The night is cool and safe. I want to sit quietly in this cockpit and let the realization of my completed flight sink in. . . . It's like struggling up a mountain after a rare flower, and then, when you have it within arm's reach, realizing that satisfaction and happiness lie more in the finding than the plucking. Plucking and withering are inseparable. . . . I almost wish Paris were a few more hours away. It's a shame to land with the night so clear and so much fuel in my tanks.

Charles Lindbergh

SEASONS OF HOPE

SIGNS OF HOPE

A message of optimism and hope is part of the rich legacy left us by one of our greatest novelists.

To wake on a summer morning with the idea of running and winning is not what any diagnostician would predict to be the upshot of an international malaise and the rumor of terminal war. I am at that age when my optimism is in danger of sounding like a greeting card or a Chinese fortune cooky. But to wake with an idea of running and winning is what I find in that generation who, in the past, would have been described as lost. Very old men and women can still be heard saying that Daddy lost everything in the crash. A whole generation of American novelists and poets exiled themselves unhappily to Europe because their native land had lost its sense of beauty. The hopeless lostness of Western Civilization was explained to us all by Arnold Toynbee and Oswald Spengler. However, one finds today a generation who see how erroneous and sentimental is the comparison between the iridescence of civilization and the passing of the light. We find mature men and women in numbers large enough to populate a small city who wake in the morning with the idea of running and winning.

In those cities where I am most disposed to feel like a wayfarer — those places where the language, the history and sometimes even the weather refresh my lingering sense of alienation — I always used to look on the streets for lovers to remind me of the universality of our experience. Men and women with their arms around one another's waists were what I looked for in Bucharest and Tallinn, in Paris and Sofia. I remember lovers on the Gianicolo Hill in Rome whose ardor seemed heightened by the newsboys who were predicting the conflagration of the planet. In countries where nothing else seemed consecutive the lovers were what I found most cheerful. This was until I saw five runners crossing in front of the Kremlin in Red Square.

One of the clichés of Eastern Europe — fortified by its history and its literature — is that sinister shadow or phantom who follows us wherever we go. The most guileless tourist in Moscow, buying a souvenir ashtray, feels that he is being tailed. A more deeply incised cliché perhaps are the towers of St. Basil's Cathedral in Moscow seen at dusk in a light fall of snow. These seemed cut into my memory at the same stratum where I find the pyramids of Gîza and the Statue of Liberty. All of this contributed to my excitement when I saw these five joggers.

Their pursuit couldn't possibly have been political or Machiavellian. They ran independently and in different directions. They followed no one nor were they followed. They gave to the gloom of Red Square a blitheness that dispersed the ancient legends of intrigue and conspiracy. They pursued some pure and unchallengeable horizons of their own that involved an improved sense of well-being and a refreshment of their earnestness. They seemed to me even more persuasive than the lovers. I began then to look for joggers, and I found them in Leningrad and Tbilisi, in Tokyo and Cairo. When, driving from the airport to a hotel in Toronto one winter's night, I saw no joggers, I went out onto the street after dinner and walked until I had discovered three of them. They seemed to declare that the best of the planet is enduring.

Because of my interest in running I recently went to see a 10,000-meter race in the country, near where I live. It was a splendid summer day, and the contestants and the observers were as comely and homogeneous a crowd as I have ever seen. The gathering looked a little like those paintings of the regatta at Cowes a century ago, but here was a homogeneity without the force of a royal family and without the power of untaxed wealth. There were no prizes, trophies or opportunities involved, and the hundreds of men and women who ran were there because it pleased them. I knew no one in the race, and when I asked the stranger beside me on the bleachers if he had come to root for a friend he seemed reluctant to answer. When I pressed him, he said: "I am rooting for my mother." It was the kind of race in which the only classification seemed to be aspiration.

Estrangement — painful estrangement — is a consequence of the truly improvisational nature of our economy, the vulnerability of our leaders to assassination and the anxiety that, in a world that seems truly bounteous — where bounty is spelled out by the very blue of the sky — it is possible for a mature and intelligent man to fail at protecting his wife and children from hunger, cold and homelessness. That we are an estranged people seems some part of our mortality — our fall from paradise — and while competitive degrees of estrangement accomplish nothing, the loneliness of our time has its singularity. We seem to be a lonely people. The understandable parochialism of the military has had to encompass the destruction of the planet; and while a computer-selected population will be lifted away from the conflagration, even the military admit that this will be a lonely parting.

My generation saw a world exposed to a much less gruel-

degenerated into a habit as accepted as the idiosyncracies of a partially broken toaster. Dinner at Mother's every Sunday? The same seat at the table every mealtime?

In every life, there are taken-for-granteds, expectations, obligations. How many of them have simply existed, unexplored, over a decade? What would happen if we left the dishes in the sink? Or if we said no?

The unexamined routines sit there like old wedding presents that no one mentions, no one likes, no one gets rid of. They take up the room we need for the new in the year.

If we resolve to sort them out and send the useless baggage off, then we have a space for risk. Then we can resolve to take a chance. To reach out. To try something we can't yet do. To surprise someone. Even to discover that some of the obligations and expectations and taken-for-granteds are really voluntary pleasures.

Enough. I have a list to make. I think I will start it again and call it "Resolutions for a Relatively New Year." I will list only one thought: Break a Pattern.

Ellen Goodman

THE FLOWERS WILL BE THERE

Wind would whip at the frail stems in the garden, but the old man knew they would stand their ground. He could do no less.

I stood on the porch of our house one day; my grandson was at my side. Below us was the tidal cove of our coastal river in Maine. When the tide is falling a shelf of rocks is exposed, and on bright days seals hunch their way out of the cold water to warm themselves in the sun. Such was the case as I stood with my grandson. Nearby, ducks paddled in the shallow waters. There were sea gulls and herons, crows and chickadees about; the life and activity and rebirth of spring.

All this was new and different to my grandson. He is from a city far away. I handed him my old binoculars, and he gazed at the seals and the ducks and the gulls, sweeping the glasses this way and that. Then, as kids do, he reversed them. Now things that were so near were far away. It delighted him. He laughed and pointed. "Those seals are a million miles away," he cried.

The long view. Look over the horizon. The eyes of youth see visions I no longer see. "When I grow up I'm going to be a major–league pitcher." "I'm going to be a doctor." Ah, when I grow up . . . 20 years, 25, 40. Old age does not grant that luxury.

We golden–agers hold the glasses and focus them so that the view of distant things is clear and close. We plan for today, for tomorrow, next month, even next year. But there is always the silent proviso: *if* all goes well.

We think of old sweet times, old frustrations. Loves that were won — and lost. We think of things that should have been done today; we'll attend to them tomorrow . . . .

Tomorrow? How many tomorrows are left? For somewhere out there lies the unfathomable — death.

It is long past midnight, and the old man who thinks these thoughts sits with a book in his lap. But he isn't reading. He stares past the lamp at his side. It is cold, and he shudders deeper into his bathrobe.

The old man finds it difficult to sleep some nights, particularly in the winter when the cold is penetrating and the footing outside is treacherous. So little chance to exercise anymore. A fall on the ice could mean a broken hip, pneumonia, perhaps the end. As a child he looked at old people and wondered why they were so careful about their health. After all, they'd lived their lives. They'd raised their families. What was there for old people to live for?

The old man thinks about that. When there is plenty of wine in the bottle one can afford to be prodigal with it. Give it away, waste it, drink too much of it. But life to the old is like the last few drops in the bottle—precious. Yes, he nods his head, that is it. With each passing day life becomes more precious.

The old man shifts in his chair. Like a honeybee in a garden, visiting first this flower, then that, his memory takes him to a birthday, a funeral, a Christmas Eve of long ago; then, to an evening last September, when he had stood at the edge of his flower garden. Not his, really. It belonged to his wife. She could make a flower bloom in soil that weeds themselves would scorn.

On that chill, late-September evening, the old man had raised his eyes to the hills in the distance. The rounded tops of the distant tiers were bathed in alpenglow, with mauve shadows blanketing the valleys. Behind and far away he heard the roll of thunder. His eyes dropped to the panoply of color at his feet. Strange, he muses now, each head seemed turned toward him. These slender, fragile things.

A storm might come tonight. Wind would whip at the frail stems and gossamer faces. But come thunder, lightning and slashing rain, these creations of some unseen Being would stand fast. They would be there in the morning! 84

That evening in his garden, with all the beauty of the world at his feet, it came to him. If these tiny, blessed flowers could stand their ground, he could do no less . . . .

"That was certainly some sigh."

"Oh, did I sigh? I wasn't aware."

We sit together in the evening; my wife there in her chair, I in mine. She is knitting me *another* sweater. How many sweaters, I wonder, has she made me through all these years? And I've worn them all, some until they've gone threadbare and disreputable. Even then it's taken my wife to discard them. Why, if it were up to me I would have a closet full of sweaters, raveled, gone at the elbow, paint-stained. She made them all.

I gaze at her. Forty-seven years. Could it be 47 years that she has been there, always close by, always there like a strong reed when I've needed help?

She was so beautiful! Her hair was the color of wheat; and like a wheat field in a summer's breeze, her hair flowed back over her head, down her back to her shoulders, where it was loosely curled. Her skin was fair, but it always wore a light tan, summer or winter. She *is* so beautiful!

The needles stop clicking. She is looking at me.

"You really should write to Ben," she says. "It's been almost a month now since you had that long letter from him."

Ben. "Yes, I'll write to him tonight."

"And that birch tree out back. You've been waiting to make sure it was dead before you cut it down."

"You think it's dead?"

"Well," she says dryly, "it hasn't had a leaf the last two summers."

I smile at her. "I'll do it in the morning."

"Good. And one more thing . . . "

I groan. "Cutting down that tree and sawing it up is all I can handle."

"I know," she says softly. "But just one more thing. . .

you've needed a haircut for two weeks now." We both laugh.

The horizon. Don't go looking over it, I think. Take the binoculars from your grandson. Look through them the proper way. The way the Lord intended them to be used. Bring the far shore up close. Write that letter. Cut down that tree. Get that haircut. Don't feel sorry for yourself. And remember, tomorrow morning the flowers will be there!

James A. McCracken

There are no hopeless situations;
there are only people who
have grown hopeless about them.

Clare Boothe Luce

THE EARTH NEVER CHANGES

Some things will never change. The voice of forest water in the night, a woman's laughter in the dark, the clean, hard rattle of raked gravel, the cricketing stitch of midday in hot meadows, the delicate web of children's voices in bright air — these things will never change.

The glitter of sunlight on roughened water, the glory of the stars, the innocence of morning — these things will always be the same.

All things belonging to the earth will never change — the leaf, the blade, the flower, the wind that cries and sleeps and wakes again, the trees whose stiff arms clash and tremble in the dark — these things will always be the same, for they come up from the earth that never changes.

Thomas Wolfe

Once, after driving all night, I passed by the restaurant in the next village over. The sun was just coming up, and the early indications were that it would be a flawless spring day, the kind a friend of mine said was reserved for the praise of poets and the forgiveness of fools. As I passed by, an old farmer came out of the restaurant, fueled by a plateful of Mrs. Barkley's good biscuits, no doubt. He looked at the sky and across the freshly plowed bottom lands, kicked up his heels and yelled, "Yaaaaa-hooooo!" Then he climbed into his old pickup and roared off into the sunrise.

John Baskin

THE LAND REMEMBERS

Mother died the winter I was 16. There was no warning. The winter itself—the same winter that always killed her fall flowers and sent her birds away—caused her death. She fell on the ice and broke her leg. Dr. Farrell came. He growled at her, put a cast on her leg and told her to rest. Before his horse was out of sight, she was already running the house from her bed. The door to her room stayed open, and her voice carried through the house. Our voices carried back to her, so she felt a part of things.

Two weeks later she woke Father in the night, saying she felt faint. He called Dr. Farrell, but in a few minutes she was dead. The rest of us were still sleeping. Dr. Farrell said a blood clot had broken loose from the area of the fracture and stopped her heart.

The weeks crept by. The hushed and whispering feel of death went away, but the house stayed quiet and empty. A thousand times I started out to look for her, to tell her something, to ask her something. In the evening, at the dining-room table, one of us would suddenly raise his head from whatever he was doing and look around, still surprised to find the empty chair at the end of the table nearest the kitchen. Father, my three older brothers and I could not believe that she was gone. Even with the constant flow of the seasons on our Wisconsin farm to remind us, we had forgotten that life is filled with endings and beginnings.

As the winter went on, there were two things I began to dread: the next blizzard and the arrival of spring. The blizzard came a month later. I woke in the night, the heavy covers pushing me down, the air in the bedroom cold on my face. The windows were rattling. That odd, deep howling of the wind was coming from the eaves along the west side of the house.

I waited, shivering. The other sound began. The piano

was humming, imitating the wind. I listened, and waited for the hair to rise on the back of my neck. It didn't happen, for the sound wasn't lonely or ghostly at all. I stopped shivering, pulled the covers up tight around me and went back to sleep, thinking of Mother singing and playing at the piano.

The days lengthened. The snow began to melt. In the house, Easter lilies bloomed, bright yellowish-white. The birds returned. The land warmed in the sun, as it had in other springs. The green came again.

Nothing had been said about a garden. One Saturday morning at breakfast, I asked our farmhand, Lyle, to get the ground ready. Everyone stopped eating. We all looked at Father. He put his hands up to his face and didn't speak. "All right," Lyle said. He smiled, the first one I'd seen from him in a long time.

Lyle began on the garden; first a load of manure, then the walking plow. I dug through the pantry and found the cardboard box with all the packets of seeds. Mother had written little notes to herself on the envelopes which held seeds we had harvested ourselves. They all made sense except one. It said, "Try a half-row, next to the larkspur. Not blue??"

I went outside with the box of seeds, the string and the garden tools. The moist dark soil was already warming in the sun, sending up the fresh smell that said *seedtime*. Without thought, I began to follow the pattern of other years.

I planted radishes, lettuce, turnips, beets and beans, working my way slowly toward the south end. I didn't know yet whether I was going to plant any flowers.

The soil went on warming in the sun, beginning to have a lighter color on the very top as it dried out a little. The knees of my trousers were damp. The mysterious living seeds passed through my fingers, one by one.

89   Finally, there was only the space at the south end where

the flowers had always been. I looked at it, lying smooth and undisturbed, and knew I couldn't leave it that way. I got the dry and shriveled dahlia tubers and gladiolus corms from the cellar. Even as I put them carefully into the ground, I couldn't quite believe that life was stored inside, waiting for a chance to come out.

I went next to the annual flowers, and first the larkspur. Had she liked it so much because of the word "lark" in the name? I had never thought about that. I planted the half-row of mystery seeds next to the larkspur, then the cosmos, zinnias and nasturtiums. Last of all, I sprinkled the tiny black seeds of rose moss and patted them into the ground with a board.

Then I started crying. I climbed high into the white-pine tree, up to my special whorl of limbs. Curled around the trunk the way I'd done when I was younger, with the branches of the big maple reaching out toward me, I let go and, for the first time, cried without trying to stop.

I had not entirely lost her after all. The seeds germinated. Neat rows of new green pushed up in the garden.

The land remembers.

Ben Logan

WALKING HOME

I was going to take the bus
  and then I didn't,
  because I didn't
  have the money.
I mean, I had the money but I didn't
  think I ought to spend it.
The fare's fifty cents now,
  half a dollar,
  half *of* a dollar,
  and for someone of my means
  (or lack of means)
  that's a lot.
So I said to myself,
"All right, I'll hike."
I wasn't looking forward to it
  though,
  I was a little tired,
  and I figured I'd be bored.
Putting one foot in front of the
  other isn't the most interesting
  thing in the world
  when you've gone the route
  a hundred times
  or more before.
And then You put on that light show,
  God.
It was beautiful, the sky
  all apricot and gold, the trees
  silhouetted.
In the space of an hour,
  light wheeled, danced and was done
  and one star shone.

91   It would be an understatement to

say
I'm glad I decided to walk home
today.
And if I tried to say anything
about Your goodness and glory,
I'd have to shout and sing,
which I'm not about to do.
Ecstasy is not a thing
folks understand
in a fellow who happens to be
seventy-six,
which I happen to be.
But, God, sometimes, between me and
You,
I'm singing-shouting glad to be
alive.

Elise Maclay

I'D PICK MORE DAISIES

Of course, you can't unfry an egg, but there's no law against thinking about it.

If I had my life to live over, I would try to make more mistakes. I would relax. I would be sillier than I have been this trip. I would be less hygienic. I would go more places. I would climb more mountains and swim more rivers. I would eat more ice cream and less spinach. I would have more actual troubles and fewer imaginary troubles.

You see, I have been one of those fellows who live prudently, hour after hour, day after day. Oh, I have had my moments. But if I had it to do over again, I would have more of them—a lot more. I never go anywhere without a thermometer, a map, a raincoat and a parachute. If I had it to do over, I would travel lighter.

If I had my life to live over, I would start going barefoot a little earlier in the spring and stay that way a little later in the fall. I would have more dogs. I would keep later hours. I would have more sweethearts. I would fish more. I would ride more merry-go-rounds. I would go to more circuses.

In a world in which practically everybody else seems to be consecrated to the gravity of the situation, I would rise to glorify the levity of the situation. For I agree with Will Durant, who said, "Gaiety is wiser than wisdom."

If I had my life to live over, I'd pick more daisies.

Don Herold

ACKNOWLEDGMENTS

Grateful acknowledgment is made to the following organizations and individuals for permission to reprint.

"First Love" by Lawrance Thompson. © 1967 by The Reader's Digest Assn., Inc.; "A Valentine Story" ("Roses Are Red") by JoAnn Dolan. Shore Line Times, February 1975. © 1975 by JoAnn Dolan; Oren Arnold in The Kiwanis Magazine, October 1964; "Our Affair By Phone" ("An Affair By Phone") by James Lees-Milne, Hamish Hamilton Ltd., London; Nikki Giovanni in Ebony, August 1981; "The Perfect Gift" ("A Gift For Mother's Day") by Ken Weber. The Rhode Islander, May 1977. Reprinted by permission of The Providence Journal-Bulletin; No Easy Victories by John W. Gardner, edited by Helen Rowan, Harper & Row, New York; A Bright and Beautiful Christmas by James Herriot. © St. Martin's Press, Inc., New York. Copyright © 1973, 1974 by James Herriot; "The Summer I Learned to See" by Jean Bell Mosley. © 1977 by The Reader's Digest Assn., Inc.; John MacNaughton in Pulpit Digest, May 1967; "A Football for Grandma" by Allan Sherman. © 1960 by The Reader's Digest Assn., Inc.; "The Grass Catcher" by Thomas Fitzpatrick. © 1978 by The Reader's Digest Assn., Inc.; "Gift From the Attic" by Ethel Salter Gayle. © 1978 by The Reader's Digest Assn., Inc.; "Pearl Diver" ("More Precious Than Pearls") by Mel Ellis. © 1971 by Wisconsin Tales and Trails, Inc.; "Season of the Empty Nest" by Joan Mills. © 1981 by The Reader's Digest Assn., Inc.; Stillmeadow and Sugarbridge by Gladys Taber and Barbara Webster, Lippincott, New York; Fonda: My Life as told to Howard Teichmann. The New American Library, Inc., New York; "Hurray! It's Raining!" by Elizabeth Starr Hill. © 1967 by The Reader's Digest Assn., Inc.; "Riches" by Katharine G. Shelly. © 1969 by The Reader's Digest Assn., Inc.; "Key to Happiness" from The Life of Alice Freeman Palmer by George Herbert Palmer. Copyright 1908, 1924 by George Herbert Palmer. Copyright renewed 1936. Reprinted by permission of Houghton Mifflin Company, New York; "Joy and Pain" by Eda LeShan. Woman's Day, October 1980. © 1980 by Eda LeShan; Russell Baker in The New York Times. Reprinted with permission; "Hyacinths to Feed the Soul" by Carol Amen. St. Joseph's Magazine, April 1968. © 1968 by Mount Angel Abbey, Inc.; Abbey Press; "Joy Along the Way" by Jean Bell Mosley. © 1978 by The Reader's Digest Assn., Inc.; My First Summer in the Sierra by John Muir. Copyright 1911 by John Muir. Copyright 1916 by Houghton Mifflin Company. Copyright renewed 1939 by Wanda Muir Hanna; "The Rarity of June" from Ox Bells and Fireflies by Ernest Buckler. Copyright © 1968 by Ernest Buckler. Reprinted by permission of Curtis Brown Ltd., New York and McClelland and Stewart Ltd., Toronto; "A Whisker of Pride" by Mary Roelofs Stott. © 1979 by The Reader's Digest Assn., Inc.; Shirley MacLaine; Charles Lindbergh from The Spirit of St. Louis. Copyright 1953 Charles Scribner's Sons, copyright renewed 1981 by Anne Morrow Lindbergh. Reprinted with the permission of Charles Scribner's Sons, New York; "Signs of Hope" by John Cheever.

Book design by Victoria Lange
Interior illustrations by Victoria Lange
Jacket art by Susan Swan
Book type set in Goudy Old Style